Dedication:

This book is dedicated to:

All of the pioneers and visionaries of every age
who chose to sail into uncharted waters.

The work of Abraham-Hicks,
for showing me that all of the outrageous,
seemingly illogical things I felt and thought
from the time I was a child were indeed my path
to true "happily ever after" NOW.

YOU
for having the courage to walk the road less traveled
and become MORE!

My Intention:

It is my intention that this book be a catalyst that ignites a fire of joy
within YOU...

...and sparks a desire for enjoying EVERY step of the journey

– because the Journey IS the Destination!

Appreciation:

I could fill 100 volumes and beyond with appreciation, as EVERY human being who has crossed my path has helped to lead me to where I am today, but as books are finite, here are some key people:

The Divine Deliberate Creators & Awesome Allowers in My Life:

My Goddess friends and Spirit Family (in no particular order): Debby Kohler, Afsaneh Noori, Magda Santos, Joanne Weiland, Cathy 'M$ Mermaid' Carey, Karen 'The Diva' Thurgood, Kathy Perry, Diane Marie, Loretta Pickford, Venus Jones, Carole 'Hummingbird Mojo Sister' Schaefer, Roger 'Mojo' Meinke, Dennis 'Starwolf', David Glass, Máire 'Fiddle Goddess' Egan, Lori 'Loretta' Ballard, Sandy Krueger the many beautiful members and wonderful new friends of our Law of Attraction Music, Media and Events Meetup.com group and all of the beautiful human beings who have crossed my path and shared their many amazing and inspiring stories of Allowing success!

My Family of Heritage & Life:

My mom, Sylvianna Romano, Ph.D., my brother Anthony Ray 'Spiritdancer' Edwards, Dolores 'Aunt Dee' Tanico, and my cousin Kathleen Fergus. Family on the other side: Nanny (Rose Romano), my brother Bruce Kenneth Satterfield, my uncle Frankie (Frank Mascari), Charles 'Carl' Lipschitz, Jennifer Renee Hartmann and all those I love eternally. My awesome second mom, Bonnie 'Hartmann' Taylor (because "mother-in-law" just doesn't fit!), my new family: Dad (Florian Sowinski) and step-mom/bonus-mom Irene Everett, and our children: Sean Michael Hartmann, Jacqualine 'Jackie' Albritton and Carey Hartmann for their part in fueling the fire of my desire to Allow and what knowing them has taught and continues to teach me.

Our Animal Teachers:

cky, AKA 'Beginner's Luck,' for being my live-in Zen Master, writing buddy d such a wonderful catalyst for so much joy and love for so many years, ` whispering in Magic's ear to show up on our doorstep to continue your ¡acy in her own unique way, and for leading us to lovable Music (my Mu!)—therefore having Magic and Music inspire me every day! The sdom of rabbit, cardinal, turtle, eagle, woodpecker, butterfly, dragonfly, ummingbird, squirrel and many others for their great reminders and ¿ssages that help keep me on an Allowing path.

My Favorite Traveling Companion:

` true love, soul-mate, play-mate, husband, best friend, fellow adventurer, eerleader, muse, lover, mirror, and "My Holiday", m Victor Hartmann:

ve you beyond measure and thank you most of all for inspiring me to low my visions and set sail with nothing but my own star to guide me. ank you for all you have added (and continue to add) to our music, ojects, and the song in my heart. Thank you for always encouraging me fully explore this uncharted yet magnificent terrain of a life of Allowing we expand our experience of joy—together.

Table of Contents

I.
Allowing Your Success: Introduction

1. Allowing: What is it and why do it?

From MAKING it happen to LETTING it happen!

Allowing: an evolution revolution!

What if you could achieve REAL success in ALL areas of your life through *letting* it happen rather than *making* it happen? What if acquiring what you truly want could feel more like a FUN adventure—such as hiking through beautiful terrain or taking a road trip on a scenic highway—on the way to your destination? What if the more joy, peace and freedom you feel NOW actually ACCELERATED the having and doing of all your deepest heart's desires?

There was a time (not very long ago) when I would have simply dismissed this as mere whimsy or wishful thinking. After encountering the work of Abraham-Hicks (www.Abraham-Hicks.com), hearing stories from real people and seeing proof of this phenomenon in action while examining my OWN life, I discovered this was not only possible, but also the surest, most joy-filled, fun and FASTEST way to TRUE success!

For years, like most "human-runnings," I felt I had to work hard and sacrifice to have success in any area of my life. I was extremely driven and proud of being a do-er, the person who would do whatever was necessary to get the job done and come Hell or High Water, *make* it happen. The problem was that Hell AND High Water usually DID come, and I faced the classic ten miles uphill, barefoot in the snow ego-glory story!

Even though I did eventually get some version of whatever it was that I wanted, I was so bloody and bruised by the time I summited the mountain that my celebration time was short and fleeting at best. Then, after a few seconds of a feeble-sounding "Yay! I did it!" followed by a collapse in some form or another, I was now looking up at the next mountain – which was twice as tall and laden with more layers of Hell AND High Water! Sound familiar?

After repeating this pattern 10,000 times too many, I decided there HAD to be another way that could include:

- more happiness.

- the excitement and challenge I liked, but without the **HHW** (**H**ell and **H**igh **W**ater).

- the FEELING of joy, success and freedom that I was hoping to get some day TODAY AND NOW.

As I put forth this inquiry, I got my answer in one beautiful word:

ALLOWING.

What is Allowing?

Simply put, Allowing is our ability to receive what we want or the ability to LET GOOD HAPPEN.

It is the key that determines the difference between forever wanting and missing versus BEING, DOING or HAVING. It is the part of the equation that makes life feel more like the fun adventure or treasure hunt it is SUPPOSED to be, rather than the struggle or arduous climb **(HHW)** that so many of us have experienced. It is feeling the FEELING that we think that our goal, dream or experience will give us eventually NOW - and then still getting all of the cool stuff and experiences we REALLY want at the IDEAL time! It is acting from inspiration rather than out of obligation. It is aligning, harmonizing and getting in sync with our visions, therefore enjoying every sweet, spectacular mile of the journey!

<u>In other words, Allowing is what it feels like when we are fully alive and in love with life.</u>

HOW do you Allow?

There are two ways to Allow:

1. *Feel Good and Enjoy the Journey*
2. *Expand/Upgrade Beliefs (Believing it IS Possible for YOU)*

As you can imagine, feeling good is certainly the easiest (and most fun!) side of the coin to embrace, so I have dedicated Section IV to techniques I have successfully used and tested which can help you to develop what I call a good **REP** or **R**epeating **E**motional **P**attern (more about **REP** in Section III, Chapter 1).

Because expanding/changing beliefs is such an über-powerful way to Allow, Sections III and IV of the book are also chock-full of insights and ideas to help you along in your journey of upgrading beliefs. I have also included:

- a super-duper tool for upgrading beliefs. (Section IV, Chapter 8)

- a link to interviews and stories from other real-life Allowers. (Section IV, Chapter 9)

- a special challenge to aid YOU in discovering your OWN Allowing evidence and give your logical mind proof that Allowing success IS ABSOLUTELY POSSIBLE for you, and infinitely more fabulous, efficient and rewarding than **HHW!** (Section IV, Chapter 9)

When you COMBINE the two keys for allowing success:

Feel Good and Enjoy the Journey + Expand/Upgrade Beliefs (Believing it IS Possible for YOU)

This is the stuff that quick manifestation and REALIZED DREAMS are made of!!!

So if you are truly ready to walk the road less traveled and unlock the magic that is your life, prepare to open your heart and mind to welcome a whole new way of living!

One word of caution...

Just as Dorothy would be forever changed after her Technicolor® trip to Oz (as was Judy Garland's real-life career!), there is no turning back. Once you experience the exhilaration of a life of ever-expanding Allowing, you will have very little tolerance for the world of black and white. You will raise your standards so much that you will become keenly aware the very moment you begin to push against the flow of life and resisting will feel far more intense than ever before.

The wonderful gift in this, however, is that any time you approach the crossroads, you will always know which way leads to the Emerald City and which points toward **HHW**-meaning you will never again unknowingly wander into a life of limitation and lack. You will have the power to live the life you have imagined on multiple levels and feel the kind of bliss and connection that IS your birthright, and in so doing, be a true inspiration to others and a real agent of global transformation!

What about the others—my partner, my family, my co-workers, people in general?

Because conscious Allowing is contrary to what many (and I dare say most) people feel and do, you may find yourself feeling like the proverbial salmon at times. The upshot here is that as you stand your ground, keeping your joy and well-being as your top priority, those who are adamant about forcing the flow of life will become less and less pronounced in your personal experience and may even disappear from your life entirely. Your joyful countenance will actually elicit more positive thoughts, feelings and actions from those around you, while drawing an ever-increasing number of like-minded people TO you!

The Bottom Line on Allowing: Do I wake up one day and Allow everything all the time?

The short answer:

As long as you remain conscious of your thoughts, feelings and intentions, and consistently choose what feels good at any given moment, it is certainly possible to live in the zone most of the time every day.

On the other hand...

Because our egos develop a few non-Allowing habits over the span of our lives—like comparing ourselves to others, focusing on things we don't like, or re-living and analyzing that unpleasant experience we had 5,000 times—the speed at which we Allow something into our life is directly related to the amount of resistance we currently hold on that particular topic. Just like Einstein would say, it's all relative. The things we believe ARE possible for us that we generally feel neutral or good about tend to show up quickly. In contrast, intentions that don't yet feel real to us or that activate more of a noticing of their absence can keep us apart from our desired result *indefinitely.*

Take heart, however! The awesome part is that the more you play with some of the tools in this book, upgrade your beliefs and make feeling BETTER your M.O., your good days will increase, your down moments will decrease, and your bling, soul mate, cash flow, fab bod, hot rod and Divine appointments will begin to materialize before your eyes and BLOW YOUR MIND as you get more and more (as Madonna would say) into the groove!!

So, are you ready to step into Technicolor and see what lies behind door #2?

CONGRATULATIONS and WELCOME BACK!!

2. Success: The New Paradigm

From Destination Fixation to ENJOYING the Journey!

Conventional Success—The Old Paradigm:
Destination Fixation

As many of the hallmarks of success have morphed and evolved over the years, the only thing that is certain in the realm of conventional success is CHANGE.

In the agricultural age, success was defined as having a booming crop, being able to get a fair trade for the (literal) fruits of one's labor, producing lots of healthy children (AKA free help) and feeding one's family.

In the industrial age, success meant producing more products faster than anyone else, and that whoever put in the longest workday won. Even wealthy inventors and business owners like Thomas Edison and Dale Carnegie prided themselves on their grueling hours and schedules.

In modern times, many of us have defined success as acquiring lots of stuff, getting on the VIP list, having a beautiful physique and being surrounded by beautiful people.

Not surprisingly, the belief about the how part of success has changed little: Work hard, get rewarded. No wonder so few people know how to consciously Allow success!

As things have started to shift economically and spiritually on a global level, many have discovered that the old ideas about success and how to go about getting it no longer seem to be producing the results that they once did. For that matter, achieving conventional success alone has rarely led to "happily ever after" and many potentially joyful nows are lost in the name of "destination fixation."

Authentic Success—The New Paradigm: Enjoying the Journey

After delving deeply into my own desires and definition of success, I discovered that every single intention I currently have—or have ever had—is based around one thing and one thing only, fulfilling what I call the **BPI** (**B**ig **P**icture **I**ntention) which is:

I am LOVING ME and having a GREAT TIME while BECOMING MORE!

While all of us have unique wants and our own personal definition of success may vary widely (hence the title, *ALLOWING Your Success!*), what good is rocking a fit and strong body, keeping up with a spiritual practice, finding our soul-mate or being a great parent if we have yet to ever truly love and respect ourselves? What value is there in having zillions of dollars or being a philanthropist if our perpetual NOW is laced with struggle and sacrifice? What joy would there be if we got everything we wanted all at once and there was nothing else to ever want, do or get excited about ever again? Every single goal is based on a result of feeling good (or simply better) about ourselves, experiencing some level of joy and expanding our horizons—in other words, *ENJOYING the journey.*

Self-love IS Success. Joy IS Success. Adventure and Expansion IS Success.

We are moving into a new era for humanity where so many things about our lives and the way we live can and will change. Getting to the heart of who we truly are, why we are really here and what is indeed meaningful to each of us is by far the best way to create and enjoy a lasting, ever-increasing success that transcends conditions. Isn't it about time to start enjoying this fantastic trip around the sun in the Age of Aquarius?

The Bottom Line on Success: The New Paradigm & the NEW Math

Don't get me wrong, I love my bling and deeply enjoy having and doing all-things-fabulous, but now that my eyes have been opened to knowing that the journey IS the destination and that success can be enjoyed and experienced EVERY day, life has become far more meaningful, far more prosperous and far more magical than I ever dreamed possible!

If you would like to expand your definition of success, try the new math:

If

The Journey = The Destination

and

The Destination = Success

then

ENJOYING The Journey = SUCCESS!

II.
Allowing Options:

Ideas for Working with this Book

Allowing Options:
Ideas for working with this book

You have options!

Since this book was written as a tool for YOU, how you choose to work with it is entirely up to YOU! Because the journey IS the destination, reading this book with an Allowing spirit (doing what feels good to you) is a great way to get the most from it. Although I have some ideas and options below, ALWAYS follow your gut and do what feels best to you at any given moment, for that is your indication that you are on to something that makes sense for YOU!

Here are some ideas for experiencing optimal Allowing:

1. Read the book from cover to cover to get a great overview, then re-read slowly.

    Pick one Positivi-T™ (Section IV—Allowing Keys & Power Tools) to play with for 30 days to easily integrate a new habit or idea into your life. For example:

    If the idea of creating a quieter mind and generally enjoying your NOW feels really good to you, focus on The Power of PRESENCE and pick one tool that also resonates.

    Because all Positivi-Ts have more than one tool, you can revisit that subject again later, (in this example The Power of PRESENCE), choosing to add a different tool, or play with all the tools over the course of an extended time.

2. Use The Power of Music to create feel-good anchors. Once you have read a chapter that has an associated song, visit the special website link in The Power of Music section of that chapter and play the song immediately. This will help you to really connect with the FEELING of being in the flow on that topic before moving on to the next chapter. You can also opt to play any particular song any time you need a quick feel-good boost!

3. Use the book as a guidance tool and flip to a random page to see what message or idea you're attracting today!

4. Want just meat and potatoes? Simply focus on the bullet points (= paragraph headings, The Bottom Line and the DO THIS sections of the Allowing Power Tools) in each chapter to get the concentrated version of the book or for a quick reminder of the heart of the message of each chapter.

5. Get some drumsticks and use the book as a percussion instrument, then set it down, put on your ruby slippers and sing "We're off to see the Wizard!" while twirling! *<giggle>*

The Bottom Line

Keep it light, do what feels good and have FUN with this, because doing anything to the contrary would be counterproductive to Allowing!

III.
Allowing
Foundation

*This section is designed to give you a solid foundation from which to begin constructing your Allowing skyscraper! Whether you are completely new to the Law of Attraction (**LOA**), would like a deeper understanding of what the **LOA** is, or would simply like to Allow it to work more in your FAVOR, you are sure to discover a jewel or THREE in this section.*

I also cover two surprising yet awesome (and even fun!) tools for Allowing: The Power of Words and The Power of Music, where I will share some thought-provoking scientific research and real-life examples. The best part about building with joy and fun as your foundation? No hard-hat required!

1. The Law of Attraction & BEYOND!

Keys to Becoming a Divine Deliberate Creator and Awesome Allower!

The Law of Attraction and Allowing

There is a good chance that if you have been attracted to Allowing, you may already be familiar with the "Law of Attraction" **(LOA)**—*and it's obviously working for you right now!*

Thanks to movies like *The Secret*, and *What The Bleep Do We Know?*, talk show hosts like Oprah, Ellen, and Larry King, and the myriad of amazing teachers, books and audio programs now available, many people have now been exposed to the **LOA.** Although many have come to understand it, it is still quite new to some individuals and certainly much of corporate culture. If you are also new to this concept, no worries, just keep reading!

There are also others who have grasped certain aspects of it, but who still want to get a clearer picture of how to really flow with the **LOA** and get what they want faster. If this feels like you, I've got you covered too, and Allowing will be a big player in your proverbial Super Bowl of manifestation, so stay with me!

The Law of Attraction Defined

The overall premise of the Law of Attraction is simple: Whatever we focus on increases, and we focus via thoughts, words and actions with thought leading the way. The Law of Attraction is not a fad-diet or something to be practiced, it just simply IS. Just like gravity, it can be a blessing or cause things to fall down and go boom - it just does what it does. The key is to work WITH the Law of Attraction to our best advantage.

My intention is to share a few key concepts and ideas to give you a clearer understanding of how it works and perhaps help you to gain a little more insight into some of the finer points—especially where the **LOA** applies to Allowing.

The Law of Attraction and Vibration

Here on planet earth everything that you experience is based on vibration, and not just in a *groovy-far-out-man* kind of way. You don't need to have a degree in quantum physics to know that the way our ears hear or how light appears to our eyes is the result of interpreting vibration. Though we cannot see the sound waves that are created when music is being played, or always hear electricity flow, or taste/touch/smell what makes it possible to talk on a cell phone or surf the net via WiFi, it happens all day every day all over the globe! Science is now also discovering that our THOUGHTS (along with what we perceive to be solid objects) have a certain rate of vibration that, like sound waves and electricity, can also be measured!

The cool part is, you don't have to wait to get your test results back from the lab to know what vibe you are putting out! All you need do is pay attention to the emotions you are experiencing and manifesting in the moment and you have all the data you need to know where you stand:

Feeling good = Good vibe = Moving toward good stuff!

Feeling not-so-good = Not-so-good vibe = No worries, adjust your vibe to get back to feeling better and moving toward good stuff!*

Yes, folks, emotions are a *manifestation* of thought and always show up FIRST before our things/experiences, that's why getting a handle on your vibration is so important if you want to create and Allow stuff you truly *want* into your life! The Beach Boys had it right! It really is all about "...good, good, good, good vibrations..."

*ALL of the Allowing Power Tools in Section IV are designed to help you shift your focus and your vibe, so I've got you covered, baby!

Law of Attraction in Action is Logical

One thing that all humans agree upon is the idea of cause and effect. When you have a line of dominoes and you tap on the first one (cause), if the dominoes are lined up properly, the rest will fall (effect). When someone complains all the time and embodies a predominantly negative attitude (AKA vibe) about life, they typically have quite a lot to complain about and/or always have to struggle to get or keep what they want in life. On the other hand, when you are in the presence of someone who genuinely praises and appreciates life, projects an overall attitude/vibe of positivity and self-confidence, and who truly feels that things always work out for the best, you often perceive her/him to be one of those people who were born under a lucky star! Simply observe anyone you know over a period of time and it is easy to see how her/his dominant vibe plays out in what manifests in her/his life. The votes are in: Whether you approach the LOA from a spiritual or intellectual standpoint, as Spock from Star Trek would say, it is "...quite logical."

A deeper look: The LOA and Source

There are a gazillion different ideas about who or what our Source may be, how S/He/It plays out in our lives, or if there even is such a thing. Where you stand and how you feel about this topic is a personal choice that really is no-one else's business but your own, but I will say that knowing where you are in relationship to resisting or Allowing the flow of your Life Force or Source (whatever you may perceive it to be) is a key part of your ability to Allow success.

Think of Source like a satellite or cell phone tower always broadcasting a consistent signal of well-being. When you feel good, meaning you've got good reception, life is groovy, people and things you've been looking for seem to come out of the woodwork, ideas come easily, you are naturally loving and generous, things just flow and you physically feel anywhere from deeply relaxed to highly energized. To the degree you feel less-than-good, you actually impede your ability to receive this signal; it can range from just getting sketchy reception to the extreme of being in a tunnel or "dead zone." In this case, everything feels like more of a struggle and you often have to work ten times harder to make any headway in life.

In both examples, the signal of well-being is there and just keeps doing what S/He/It does, much like the Law of Attraction. It is up to the receiver (AKA YOU) to keep your connection clear. Once you discover your own ability to tune in to the frequency of your Source and personally experience the incredible leverage that comes as a bonus, being tuned in becomes far more appealing than being tuned out! Consider this: If pain, suffering or experiencing negative emotions on a consistent basis were good for us, why is it that they lead to exhaustion, disease and a shorter life span?

Whatever your view of Source, why not opt to enjoy the journey, live the sweet life or even Allow the **LOA** to assemble a team of fabulous players and experiences that would even put JLo's entourage to shame!

21

YOU are the CEO

Divine Deliberate Creators and Awesome Allowers all have one thing in common – they have the absolute knowing that they and they alone are responsible for their own life experience and know that nothing and no-one can stop them from living a life they love. Even though a great majority do believe in some form of Source (whether they call this God, Jesus, Allah, Goddess, the Universe, the Quantum Field, full brain potential, etc.), they know that when it comes down to it, they are THE deciding factor as to whether or not they enjoy the journey. Whatever your spiritual beliefs (or non-beliefs) are, acknowledging that you are the **CEO** of your personal life experience is one of the most powerful steps you can take toward truly and fully Allowing Your Success!

You are the **C**reator, **E**xperiencer and **O**pener or **CEO.**

Creator: You create and attract through thought, and the thoughts that are the most consistent and emotionally-charged ultimately become manifestations.

Experiencer: You get to experience the result of whatever you have been creating.

Opener: You open the door (Allow) to LET what you want into your life (or not).

To be a great CEO, get a good REP!

Some folks who DO understand the Law of Attraction get a little frustrated when they feel they ARE putting thought and energy into what they want, but they actually spend a little more time on auto-pilot. They repeat old thoughts or hold on to old beliefs that are focused more on the *absence* of what they want than the *having* of it. If you've experienced anything like this and would like to start Allowing the Law of Attraction to work FOR you, all you need to do is develop a good **REP** (**R**epeating **E**motional **P**attern)!

When you prioritize feeling good and cultivate a generally good **REP** more than half of your waking time, you begin to build a level of positive momentum that affects every piece of the **CEO** equation:

- a good **REP** means you naturally think more feel-good thoughts and set the wheels in motion for feel-good CREATIONS!

- a good **REP** means you get the EXPERIENCE of feeling good now!

- a good **REP** means less resistance and more Allowing = OPENING the door for good stuff to flow!

*The Allowing Keys and Power Tools: Positivi-Ts that follow in section IV are ALL about getting and maintaining a fantastical **REP**, so read on!*

Here's a fun analogy: You've already won the lottery!

What if you received word that everything you wanted was a DONE deal? What if you knew you'd DEFINITELY won the lottery and had only one small task to do before you get it: Enjoy the journey by feeling amazing and relaxed most of your waking time, while maintaining a true attitude of "I'm fabulous with or without any of my stuff!"?

Most likely if you *knew* winning was guaranteed and that the more often you feel good and relax into that knowing, the FASTER your windfall would arrive, this would become your main focus in life, right? This, my friends, is exactly the way the **LOA** can deliver what you want quickly! How you feel now determines how you feel later and things like cash flow, great relationships and optimum health tend to visit and STAY in feel-good environments where they are welcomed and appreciated!

More about how to work with The Power of APPRECIATION in Chapter 5 of Section IV.

Keep it light for visions to take flight!

Have you noticed that the less urgency or desperation there is surrounding having or doing something, the easier the process of aligning with it is? Interestingly enough, once something becomes important and HAS to happen in order for us to feel OK, it becomes heavy, slows things down and actually ADDS resistance to letting the very thing we want into our life!

Important signifies that there is an attached consequence if it *doesn't happen*, so our focus and vibe become more about the consequences of NOT HAVING/experiencing than the joy and fun of HAVING/experiencing.

When you realize that no experience or thing defines who you are, and that you are awesomely awesome in your awesomeness no matter what, you immediately lighten your load and set your dreams, visions and SELF free to BE (as Sting would say, "If you love somebody <or dream/vision/ etc.> set them free...").

Tips and tools for lightening up are also prominent in Section IV, especially in Chapter 10, The Power of HUMOR.

<u>FIRST AND FOREMOST</u>, always remember the BPI:

"I am LOVING ME and having a GREAT TIME while BECOMING MORE."

Sometimes we get attached to a specific thing, relationship or opportunity that we think will lead us to the **BPI**, but in essence, that thing is merely a *how* rather than a destination. As mentioned in Success: The New Paradigm (Section I, Chapter 2), everything we could possibly ever want is linked to the desire and hope that said thing will make us feel good, or at least better. Enjoying the journey is THE key to being a Divine Deliberate Creator and Awesome Allower, so always keep the **BPI** front and center when considering your next object of focus and attention.

Know when you are "feeding your baby"

Sometimes when we say we want something, what we are actually thinking of and feeling is the ABSENCE of it. How many times have you heard or used "I want that SO badly, so much it hurts!"? If there is any feeling of badness around it, where you feel less or empty without it, even the most positive-sounding words cannot counteract the overall signal (vibe) of lack we are sending out. Just like you would do all you could to care for a real baby, your intentions and dreams are just as precious and deserve the same kind of love and clear focus. If you would like to see your baby/intentions grow into a healthy, thriving, full-blown creation, always pay attention to how you feel. When you're feeling good, you're feeding your baby! Otherwise...well, you get the picture!

Fill up on the good stuff—No news is good news

If what you want to feel, experience and create differs from what you see or hear on the news, TV, the papers, online or on the radio, change the channel, read something else or push the off button more often.

Here are some questions I ask myself when I run across a media blast:

1. Can I see a solution here?
2. Would I enjoy taking action and investing the time in being part of the solution?
3. How is this making me feel?

If the answers are (in sequence):

1. Yes!
2. Yes!
3. Excited and happy

I keep watching with the solution in mind.

If the answers are (in sequence):

1. Yes or No
2. No
3. Like crap

I change the channel, turn the dial, put the paper down, read something else or flip the switch to "off."

But what about being informed?

When you are conscious of the **BPI** and your specific intentions (and personal safety is just part of the package deal there), it's amazing how you always find out about anything that is important to you. It is, of course, your choice: Would you rather feed your baby by feeling good and enjoying having the things you want or cut off your baby's food supply so you can gossip and rehash with your co-workers about how the world is going to hell and keep running on the wheel with all the other hamsters? If you're undecided (not sure why...) try the "No news is good news 1-day challenge" (opt out of watching the news for 24 hours) to see if life actually goes on without it for one day.

Something to remember about the media:

The media are not Satan. They are merely fulfilling their intentions to go out and search until they find something newsworthy and dramatize it to the max to make it compelling to watch. Sometimes they bump into something positive, but because their intention is typically to look for negative extremes, that is what they find (hmmm – the intention is to look for negative happenings and that's what they find? Sounds like the Law of Attraction in action, don't you think?)

The good news!

The *good* news is there are more and more radio shows, magazines, blogs, forums, and TV shows that are emerging with a positive and inspiring focus. If you prefer to stay informed, wouldn't it be better to stay *informed of the evidence of good things* and inspiring ideas that help you live a happier, more joy-filled life?

It's OK to sleep on it

Sometimes if we feel not-so-hot and have tried every which way to feel better, but nothing seems to work, it's better to get a little shut-eye than to add fuel to an unwanted fire. Getting some rest always gives us a chance to have a do-over and start with a clean slate!

The LOA and Dreams

Here's more good news! We only actively create when we are awake, so there is no need to worry about or obsess over dreams. Though dreams are a result of the Law of Attraction in action, and yes, are also a manifestation of vibration, their main purpose is to give us a little behind-the-scenes peek into the general direction we are going—much like using Google Earth or looking at a map to see where we will end up if we stay on this particular road. If you are not diggin' the direction in which you're headed, no worries! Simply shift your focus or choose another road that moves you more toward your desired destination. 'Nuff said!

Just like re-hashing—or worse, *obsessing*—over any unpleasant conversation or experience, the yucky dreams can only negatively affect your waking experience if you give them LOTS of your conscious focus. Simply use any funky dreams (like funky emotions) for what they are - a tool to help you get back on track to focusing on the good stuff!

On the other hand, if you have fun, fabulous or even lucid dreams, focusing on those can bring some happy mojo into your conscious creating! This means you are hot on the trail of aligning with something

WAY cool, so just like awesome experiences in our waking life, really appreciating and milking the sweet dreams can also help move you closer to your heart's desires faster!

Consciousness is the KEY to being a Divine DELIBERATE Creator

If you prefer to create INTENTIONALLY rather than just have any old thing show up on your door step, keep your eyes on the road and your hands on the wheel *(Jim Morrison – quite a prophet, eh?)*. Create check points throughout your day to remember where you are, declare what it is you want and most importantly, in case I haven't mentioned this enough yet, <u>ALWAYS PAY ATTENTION TO HOW YOU FEEL!</u>

It is a lot easier to shift your thinking* (and ultimate manifestation) if you've just had ONE goofy thought that felt a little off rather than trying to shift the momentum of negative thoughts and feelings that have been building in strength for several minutes, hours or days.

How to do this? I'll share lots of ideas in Section IV!

YOU are the only one who can create YOUR life—period

Have you ever noticed that any effort to try to get someone else to do something you think they should do rarely turns out well, if it even works at all? How do you feel when you've been on the other end of that equation with well-meaning family, friends, teachers, etc. telling you how you should live your life and what you should want? I would guarantee not very warm and fuzzy!

If we were all meant to want, be, do and have all the same things, life would be as boring and unproductive as hell—illogical, really. The thing to remember is people treat us and make suggestions based on how THEY think and feel. The problem is when we decide that their view or opinion of us matters more than how we feel in our gut, we soon end up in same-and-boringville or even down in a tunnel far, far away from the nearest life-force communication tower with a serious case of amnesia and the bummers.

Wanting the best for others is certainly a wonderful thing, indeed, but it is important to know that EVERY human being on this planet is a **CEO** with her or his own Source always sending out a strong signal to guide them toward their unique style of fulfilling the **BPI**. To become dependent on another as a Source substitute will never Allow you to discover your own power. Becoming another's source of happiness will likewise never, ever Allow your fellow travelers the joy of finding their own way or remembering their own strength. This also prevents you from getting to fulfill YOUR **BPI** in your own unique, creative ways.

To best help others, BE the living example of all good things and experience your OWN Allowing evidence, because we humans love seeing tangible proof that what we want IS possible! By doing this, you then plant seeds for others to upgrade THEIR beliefs, which then helps ALL of us to Allow! By Allowing YOUR joy, you help them allow THEIRS. Talk about offering a wonderful service to humanity!

You don't have to believe a damn thing

Here's the other great part about the Law of Attraction—and any of the info presented in this book—you don't have to believe ANY of it, not one word, not one syllable, zip. There are many things in our world that function regardless of our belief in them. There are also many people who have experienced what we would call miracles that defy all logic or comprehension. This book is simply another jumping off point to help stimulate some thought, provide a few tools and laughs, and help you to remember what you already know so that YOU can then choose what to do about the information contained herein.

As much as I would enjoy the thought that this book changed your life, that you managed to attract and allow some cool stuff or that you were even able to live a happier life, it is my job and joy to Allow you to do what you will. I love and respect you as the magnificent **CEO** that you are, and in any case, I've had one heck of a fabulous time writing this book!

The Bottom Line on The Law of Attraction and Allowing

Whatever you choose to do, feel or believe, I am THRILLED for you and know that the universal Law of Attraction can be your greatest ally, if you Allow it to be.

Always remember that YOU and YOU alone are the best teacher of YOU, no matter how fabulous this book or advice being shared by any other expert with a long list of credentials may be. Choosing to follow what feels best in YOUR heart and gut at any given time is always YOUR path of least resistance to Allowing Your Success!

In the next section, I will be sharing lots of different tools for how you can work WITH the Law of Attraction, stay CONSCIOUS to create what you WANT, and most importantly, become an ever-increasing Allower!

If you would like to learn more about the Law of Attraction, below are some of my personal favorites:

Movies, Books & Beyond:

What The Bleep Do We Know?
The science behind thought (quantum physics)
presented in a fun format
www.WhatTheBleep.com

The Secret
Created by Rhonda Byrne and featuring many
of today's Law of Attraction specialists
www.TheSecret.tv

The Secret Behind the Secret
DVD Featuring Abraham-Hicks (the original inspiration behind
the Secret–only watch with an open mind)
www.Abraham-Hicks.com

You Can Heal Your Life film featuring the work of Louise Hay
www.YouCanHealYourLifeMovie.com

The Law of Attraction audio series by Abraham-Hicks
www.Abraham-Hicks.com

Ask and it is Given book/audio by Abraham-Hicks
www.Abraham-Hicks.com

The Power of Intention book/audio by Dr. Wayne Dyer
www.DrWayneDyer.com

The Secret book/audio by Rhonda Byrne
www.TheSecret.tv

Notes From The Universe and *Infinite Possibilities*
books by Mike Dooley
www.Tut.com

As a Man Thinketh by James Allen

Think and Grow Rich by Napoleon Hill

The Science of Getting Rich by Wallace Wattles

Illusions by Richard Bach

SoundsTrue.com (multiple titles, authors and resources)

HayHouse.com (multiple titles, authors and resources)

Transformation-Publishing.com (multiple titles, authors and resources)

2. The Power of Words

Talking the Talk Complements Walking the Walk

What do words have to do with Allowing?

All those who think in words or communicate through words (that would be almost all of us!) invest a great deal of time and even more importantly, EMOTION, in our spoken and unspoken lingo. Yes, there are plenty of empty words flying around, but often the things we say to ourselves and others bear fruits of truth, and can pack a punch in creating power when emotions are present.

Words are part of our creative power

We can conceive of an idea or notion in our minds, but speaking it is what converts this intangible thought form into something we can define, grasp and express, and the words we choose to use have a definite bearing on the actions we take and how we feel.

Dr. Masaru Emoto, author of *The Hidden Messages in Water*, demonstrates that attaching different words to specimens of water (via labeling the containers) causes the shape of the water crystal (when frozen) to vary. Interestingly enough, the more positively charged words such as "thank you,", "love," "appreciation," etc., created the most symmetrical and beautiful crystals, while anything to the contrary created scattered, broken forms. Knowing that our bodies and the bodies of those with whom we interact are comprised mainly of water, logic AND science now demonstrate that our words *absolutely* have an effect on our physical well-being as well as the physical well-being of others.

Since words comprise and reflect our thoughts, and thoughts create our reality, the more we use words that are in alignment with being who we truly are and living our dreams and visions, the more we attract and Allow these very things!

The Bottom Line on The Power of Words

Wouldn't it be amazing if we could simply say "abracadabra" and (poof!) get our stuff on command?! Although our words ARE indeed powerful, they are only part of the equation. They CAN, however, help each of us to develop a good **REP** (Repeating Emotional Pattern) by calling upon and stimulating emotions that feel good on a regular basis AND help us start training our minds, hearts and bodies to Allow our intentions when they show up. By focusing on these thoughts when they feel good and calling forth even more feel-good emotions, the reality of living our intentions becomes easier to accept and hence feels natural. This is MUCH more fun than the "I-can't-believe-it!-It's-too-good-to-be-true" syndrome.

Again, it's up to you, but if you're willing to vote for feeling good now and are able to graciously accept what you want when it shows up, using The Power of Words can definitely be a worth-while investment for YOU, *and* a way to positively influence others into Allowing THEIR Success!

Here's a sample of what The Power of Words for Allowing Your Success looks like:

Instead of Stone-Age Slang	Use Focused Phonics
The only way to be successful is to work hard and hope for the best.	I've noticed that when I am truly enjoying what I do, I do it better, attract happier people, get better results and get to enjoy my life NOW!
Life's a b___ and then you die.	When I see that life is a gift, then I thrive!
Success is that elusive thing that only a select few ever realize.	Success is my birthright and something I can experience today and NOW. The best part is as I feel good more and more, I receive more and more – now. THAT's what I call success!
How can I Allow when everyone wants MY stuff?!	It feels so good to know that I absolutely CAN have what I truly want, as can everyone else. I, and I alone, can choose to Allow my success and knowing I have that power feels SO good.

*To get your Power of Words groove on, each chapter in Section IV contains a table like the one above featuring examples of real life communication that can help you feel more like the **CEO** you truly are!*

For more about The Power of Words:

All books by Dr. Masaru Emoto

You Can Heal Your Life and many others by Louise Hay

The Four Agreements, Don Miguel Ruiz

3. The Power of Music

Allowing Your Success with a Great Soundtrack!

The power to time travel, transcend, transform and connect all people

How many of us have heard a certain song and were then instantly transported back in time to a specific event and place in our memories enabling us to relive that experience and emotion here and now? Have you noticed that certain songs bring tears, laughter, anger, celebration, feelings of sensuality, and calming?

Even when listening to instrumental pieces or songs in different languages, we can still get an overall feeling about that piece of music, or the overall mood, if you will. Why? Because music is UNIVERSAL. It speaks to every human being on the planet regardless of our cultural, ethnic, religious or economic backgrounds, and brings with it the power to do virtually anything with our mood and overall state of well-being.

OK, talking about The Power of Music is certainly no stretch for me, as it is one of my greatest passions in life. It is amazing, though, to be reminded of how transformational this tool can be no matter where we are in our lives and professions.

I had the honor and joy of experiencing two phenomenal concerts in February of 2008. Both were powerful, but in completely different ways, and with completely different voices and stories to tell.

Billy Joel (www.BillyJoel.com) has been one of my favorites for many years. His songs paint a picture of everyday life—some songs celebrate it, while others are purely cathartic.

Looking at a full house around American Airlines stadium in Miami and hearing thousands of voices cheering and singing songs like "Piano Man," "Scenes from an Italian Restaurant," and "New York State of Mind," almost instantly brought me back to the years I lived in my Italian neighborhood of Bensonhurst in Brooklyn, NY. I had not thought about my childhood surroundings for many years, but when my husband and I got back to our hotel that evening, I found myself giving him a tour of the old neighborhood with the help of Google Earth. While mentally traveling through time and space, I felt a whole new sense of love and appreciation for the approximate two square miles that was the focal point of my world for over twelve years of my life! All because of a few great songs.

Ladysmith Black Mambazo (www.mambazo.com) is an a capella vocal ensemble group from South Africa that first grabbed my attention while watching one of my favorite romantic comedy movies of all time, *Coming to America.* As I entered the venue to hear one of their concerts, I was floored and moved by the diversity of ages and ethnic backgrounds in the audience. It had the sense of a United Nations gathering! The music—traditional African with some pop-ish/gospel, mostly sung in the Zulu language and wrapped around a message of peace and unity—touched a deep and primal place in my soul that made me feel as if I was hearing the voice of Great Mother Earth herself—*utterly magical.* How did I feel after this concert? Connected. Mesmerized. Transformed. All because of a few great songs.

Music for Creation

When we take a comprehensive approach, the symbiotic relationship of positive, affirming words AND feel-good music creates a power-house partnership rich in potential for healing, mood shifting and even life transformation. Just as a song can evoke a memory or an overall mood by transporting us into that experience in a very visceral way, it's no stretch to conclude that listening to, singing with, dancing to or composing uplifting music carries with it great potential power. The key factor is choosing music we enjoy, since like any healing modality, receptivity is the first step in being able to truly effect a change.

The good news is once the door is open through a medium we can personally relate to and connect with (such as popular and modern styles of music like rock, pop, R & B, country and jazz), the message can find its way to our psyche and spirit by default, even if not on a conscious level. A prime example of this is illustrated by little children singing along with adult language they may not completely understand. Just as kids learn their ABC's through music, this new language also begins to translate into their world and their subconscious. "I believe the children are our future, teach them well and let them lead the way..."

The GREAT news is when we are fully aware of the words and feelings being communicated in a song and completely immerse ourselves in the positivity of a piece, the degree of emotional shift we can experience is even more pronounced!

The science of uplifting or "designer" music

A fascinating study conducted by Rollin McCraty, Ph.D., Bob Barrios-Choplin, Ph.D., Mike Atkinson, and Dana Tomasino, B.A. addresses the effects of what they call "designer" music (visit http://www.heartmath. org/research/research-papers/effect-music-mood.html for the entire article):

"This study investigated the impact of different types of music on tension, mood and mental clarity. A total of 144 subjects completed a psychological profile before and after listening for 15 minutes to four types of music (grunge rock, classical, New Age and designer). With grunge rock music, significant increases were found in hostility, sadness, tension and fatigue, and significant reductions were observed in caring, relaxation, mental clarity and vigor. In contrast, after listening to the designer music (music designed to have specific effects on the listener), significant increases in caring, relaxation, mental clarity and vigor were measured: significant decreases were found in hostility, fatigue, sadness and tension. The results for New Age and classical music were mixed. Feeling shifts among subjects were observed with all types of music. Designer music was MOST effective in increasing positive feelings and decreasing negative feelings. Results suggest that designer music may be useful in the treatment of tension, mental distraction and negative moods." [emphasis added]

Music for Allowing

I noticed that when I started writing, recording and performing music with positive messages and intentions, MY life began to be transformed in *every* aspect. I started internalizing the positive language that filled these songs and began integrating these empowering words, ideas and FEELINGS into my every day conversations and business dealings. I now find it easier to process and move past challenges by shifting my focus and mood and in so doing, consistently Allowing more opportunities for fun AND profit across the board than I have ever experienced in my life! The fact that you are reading this book is proof positive of this phenomenon in action!

The Bottom Line on The Power of Music

Feeling good is the name of the game for attracting and Allowing the good stuff, so isn't a magical life worth celebrating even more fun when accompanied by a great soundtrack?

Due to the profound experience The Power of Music has had on my life, the idea of adding something unique and FUN to this book that can pump up the volume of YOUR Allowing experience prompted me to attach feel-good songs to all of the main subjects contained herein! Having purchased this book, you will have the ability to visit a secret web page and use a special code to be able to download these fun and powerful tunes for FREE! Who loves ya, baby?!

If you would like to test the waters and get a taste of what
a life of Allowing feels like, visit this link:

www.AllowingYourSuccess.com/SecretPages

- ☛ Then use the code AYS-tjitd
- ☛ Then choose ALLOWING Music
- ☛ Then click on any song title that feels good to you!

*Thank you in advance for honoring and respecting the value
of our work and using this code just for you and your household.

IV.
Allowing Keys
&
Allowing Power
Tools:

Positivi-Ts™

In this section you will have the opportunity to play with lots of new tools for expanding your experience of Allowing. Different tools may be more effective for you at different times or even overall, so I highly encourage you to listen to YOUR inner teacher to decide which tools apply best for YOU.

I have intentionally selected twelve Positivi-Ts to give you the option of working with one subject per month. I have personally discovered that making changes in bite-sized pieces tends to be far more effective than trying to swallow an über-pie in one gulp! As mentioned in Section I (Allowing Options: Ideas for working with this book), you can also opt to simplify further by picking only one tool from each subject and really taking your time with it. There is no deadline or pressure to do anything in any allotted time because enjoying the journey IS the name of the game.

Each Positivi-T contains five different components:

1. *Allowing Keys*

2. *Allowing Power Tools*

3. *Themed Power of Words samples*

4. *Themed Power of Music songs that you can download for free by visiting the link and using the code provided*

5. *Additional Resources*

Feel free to use any or all of these components to pump up the volume on enjoying your Allowing adventure!!

Remember: the rule is that there are no rules, only a suggestion to take this all in with an open mind, an appreciative heart and an Allowing spirit.

ENJOY!

1. The Power of FOCUS: Allowing Keys

Ready to LET good happen and ENJOY the Journey?
Focus is EVERYTHING!

Every adventure first begins with a point of FOCUS and a choice

Whether you believe a pattern of choosing begins pre-birth in a non-physical waiting room of sorts or once we reach Terra firma, life as we know it is an infinite stream of choices. Whether we recognize this or not, we are perpetually choosing our point of focus. Focus is, in essence, where every journey begins, what defines our journey and our ULTIMATE power tool for Allowing success!

Focus is, in a word, EVERYTHING when it comes to Allowing success

What we focus on IS what we choose and what ultimately manifests in our life. Whatever we focus on increases. Whatever we focus on we engage. Whatever we focus on we BECOME. The fabulous news is when we take control of our power of FOCUS (the ONLY thing, by the way, we truly and absolutely CAN control), instead of being subject to the world at large, we can opt to find ourselves where we would choose to be and feel good no matter where we are standing. Think about it this way: Would you rather get in your car and drive in a random direction with a blindfold on and pray that you make it back alive or plug a destination into your GPS, follow clear guidance with your eyes open and arrive in style?

It's a no-brainer, folks, focus is where it's at!

This seems simple and logical enough, but when the whole world is passionately shouting different directions at us, or a large number of vehicles is going THAT way when our guidance says go THIS way, staying on top of our Power of FOCUS and Allowing our success can certainly be a challenge at times. It does take a degree of mental muscle and courage to listen to YOUR gut (guidance) above all else and be a Divine deliberate creator. But if letting good happen and enjoying the journey IS your M.O., it absolutely, positively CAN be done once you choose to go New School.

Enrolling in New School starts with getting committed—to JOY!

I can hear you thinking already, "What on earth does commitment have to do with Allowing?" Let me 'splain...

Are you letting your life run YOU or are YOU running your life? If you're not quite sure of the answer to this question, ask yourself, "How do I FEEL?"

If YOU are running your life: You are in the flow, feeling energized, enthusiastic, peaceful, clear, alive, etc.

If your LIFE is running you: You tend to feel overwhelmed, stressed, confused, exhausted, and generally not-so-much...

We know now that we are all **CEOs** who CREATE OUR LIFE so the idea of chasing IT, quite frankly, is like watching a dog chase its tail for hours—amusing, yes, but...

With SO much data flying around, so many options and so many different demands and expectations from others, it is no wonder we sometimes feel like we end up wherever the wind takes us. We look back thinking, "Now why did I do (or not do) THAT?" or even decide that this Law of Attraction thing is just out to get me! To fix the problem, we are told (or tell ourselves), "Suck it up!" or "Be more disciplined!" If we work harder, exercise more, do what that Terez chick thinks I should do, yadda yadda yadda then I'll get what I want. But rarely do we stick to any of these things or find ourselves where we truly want to be. This is what I call "Old School" discipline. Let me introduce you to New School (I think you're really gonna like this!).

First of all, let me preface with the statement that there are some Old School things—like great music, grand romantic gestures, timeless movies, classic cars, etc.—that are still VERY cool, but when it comes to the notion of discipline, The Power of FOCUS, AKA New School, is THE way to go bro! Check this out:

Tell me whether or not you agree with this statement:

"Gee, I SO love to suffer and endure miserable, punishing tasks so I might eventually get what I want some time before I die!!"

If you said "yes," please put this book down and immediately call the Masochist hotline. Otherwise:

Welcome to New School (AKA Enjoying the Journey!)

Now, for those who said "no way Jose!", you are a sane and wise person who has discovered a very simple truth: We rarely stick to doing things we hate. There's a reason for that—IT DOESN'T FEEL GOOD! If you've read any part of the book so far, you now know that feeling good IS the name of the game when it comes to Allowing success. Perhaps there's an innate knowing we all possess which tells us that doing this crazy thing that sucks the life out of us, stresses us out, or physically hurts us is NOT going to move us toward our happily ever after. Even the most well-meaning of us, who can and would endure for the sake of future success, eventually get to a breaking point of one kind or another.

Instead of Old School discipline mentality telling us that we're quitters and losers, New School instead says, "Bravo!!! It's about time you stopped torturing yourself and started getting back to enjoying the journey! Yay!" If you think about it, why would we ever want to waste a moment of our precious lives doing something we hate and get sketchy results when we could be doing something we LOVE and get GREAT results? This is the essence of New School and exercising our power of FOCUS. My friends, if you're going to commit to something, commit to ENJOYING THE JOURNEY, for the journey IS the destination! *(hmmm... I've heard that somewhere before...).*

New School is all about courage and character

Now I know this may be a very different idea for many of you who are reading this and you may have even gone back to read the previous two paragraphs two or three times to make sure you understood what was written on the page. A few of you may even be thinking, "If I only just do the things I love, what is the challenge in that?" I feel you, I do, but here's the thing: Choosing to commit to doing the things that keep you on track and keep your connection flowing with your Source when the rest of the world is running around screaming, *"Everything is wrong and life is hard and the sky is falling!"* while shoving newspaper clippings and funky Facebook posts in front of you is one of THE most challenging things a human can do! New School is all about exercising the ultimate power of FOCUS and deciding to follow the guidance that comes from WITHIN, regardless of what the rest of the world is doing.

New School is about courage and character. New School is about being a leader and a TRUE source of inspiration for others. It is, in essence, what we truly came here to do: Sort through the details of life, decide what lights our personal fire at any given moment, and use our brilliant and powerful mind to focus on what we want until we are at one with it, and repeat the process as we continually expand into being more and more.

Old School/New School Comparison

Want an even clearer picture of what enrolling in New School looks like? Here's a comparison:

Old School Discipline—The Funky 7:

1. Send out e-mails every five minutes and post forty things to my Facebook page every day in the hopes someone might eventually hire me or buy my stuff.

2. Go to every imaginable singles hot spot or register for every online dating company I can find to try to hunt down and hog-tie my soul-mate.

3. Do some crazy deprivation diet or brutal exercise routine to suffer my way to my ideal weight and then never Allow myself to enjoy my favorite foods again without berating myself fiercely.

4. Take every pill (even though there are 400 side-effects) or do every surgery I can in the hopes of healing/fixing/perfecting some part of my body or mind.

5. Go to every seminar, buy every book, do every exercise the "experts" advise and make sure I do my 146 action steps every day without fail so that I may someday be a better person.

6. Do all the right things so that my husband, wife, mom, dad, kids, friends, consider me to be a good person.

7. Deprive myself of the things I enjoy so I can be a good mom/dad and stay on top of what my kids are doing at every moment to make sure they never get hurt and make all the right choices.

New School (AKA The Power of FOCUS)— The Magnificent 7:

1. Start my day with appreciation, meditation and/or do things throughout the day that get my wheels turning in a good way.

2. Pay attention to how I feel at any given moment and when I feel a blip on my radar, choose a thought that feels better or go back to the good thing I was thinking about pre-blip.

3. Feel BEFORE I act. If it feels natural and good, I do it. If my gut says no-go, I listen. If it is something I feel is important to do, like paying my bills, etc., I take a few seconds (or a few minutes if necessary) to find a way to feel good before taking action for better results.

4. Get clear and go to the heart of what I truly want and why I want it and "feed my baby" with good thoughts throughout the day.

5. When I start to criticize or complain, especially out loud, I choose to praise or appreciate something else I DO like instead.

6. When I get an idea that feels amazing, I act on it as soon as possible!

7. I enjoy the journey and love my life now, for I know the journey IS the destination and Enjoying the Journey = Success!

New School/The Power of FOCUS, like authentic success, is truly a paradigm shift

Instead of doing THIS so I can get THAT, we do what feels right by enjoying the journey NOW and make that our top priority. Rather than trying to control the behavior of others or beating ourselves up enough physically and emotionally so we can feel good (taking the *Beatings will continue until morale improves!* approach), New School is an INSIDE job. It is all about exercising choice and using the power of our mind to FOCUS on the things that are life-GIVING.

Now here's an important point to make. Each of us has our own belief system in place about what it takes to have success in certain areas of life. Even those like us who are pretty solid on the path of Allowing, who see the logic of using the Power of FOCUS/New School, may still have times when we feel we really must do A to get B. In this case, it is always best to stay in integrity with our beliefs, especially if it does feel good and right to us, until we Allow a belief upgrade (more about this in Chapter 8, The Power of HARMONY). Below are some examples and ideas.

Allowing Success: Edison, Ford & Oprah—finding the love in the journey

So what about those professional athletes and amazing musicians who practice for hours and hours to become masters and champions or people like Edison or Ford or Oprah who worked crazy-long hours and paid their dues—isn't that Old School? I wondered about this for quite a while myself, but there is a way that hard work can lead to a happy destination.

All of these folks felt that in order to be great, working hard was non-negotiable, so they found a way to make peace with and even learned to LOVE the process! The more love they found and continued to find, the more authentic success they experienced (doing what they truly wanted to do with a healthy life balance). On the flip side, the less they enjoyed the journey, the harder they still had to work to stay where they were, and had other areas of their lives that were far less joyful than what they have would preferred.

I can speak only for myself, but after considering my Old School discipline days as compared to tasting the sweetness of Allowing success and embracing The Power of FOCUS/New School (which also comes with the side benefit of having more FREEDOM and no longer depending on others to make things happen for me) I very quickly decided that changing schools was well worth the trip!

How to reconcile this for yourself? Check out TOOL#4: DO WHAT YOU LOVE OR FIND THE LOVE IN IT! in this chapter's Allowing Power Tools!

The Power of FOCUS and excellence

Whether we approach success from the vantage point of Old School or New School, one thing that both schools have in common is this: Excellence is and always has been about FOCUS. All record-breaking professional and Olympic athletes, world-class musicians, actors and artists who have had the world's eyes and ears on them, have developed a phenomenal ability to stay focused on their passions both long-term and in the moment.

How do they do this? They consciously CHOOSE to focus on what matters most to them—and they keep doing it. Remember that the Law of Attraction is ALL about focus, so the more we focus upon something, the more dominant it becomes in our lives. This is what we call creating a habit, and when we are in the habit of focusing on knowing our talents, abilities, skills and visions, THAT is what manifests! Excellence in any area of life is simply a game of focus that is open to ALL players of the game of life!

New School means choosing your destination— even for short trips

Whether we walk, drive, fly, paddle, etc., we always have an intention/ destination in mind.

Even when being spontaneous, there is still an intention to see and experience something beautiful, cool, or at the very least, to enjoy the journey. Every action we take, whether it is:

- making a phone call or responding to an e-mail
- making or enjoying a meal
- going out on a date
- reading a book
- going to work out
- meeting with a client
- cleaning the house
- camping, etc.

has some kind of desired intention/result in mind. Setting an intention in advance (what Abraham-Hicks calls "segment intending"), sends the message out ahead of us and helps us focus on what we want. This gets the wheels turning to do more of the same—AND makes it far easier to relax and enjoy the journey along the way, because all that is required at this point is engaging in the present moment and following our internal navigation system!

Shift your Focus as needed

In an effort to fix a problem or make an unwanted thing go away, we humans have a tendency to heavily analyze, examine, or figure out why something has gone wrong or why that thing we don't like exists. The boo-boo here is that the more we delve into what we don't want, putting more thought into said problem, the longer we keep the funky thing and feeling alive. In fact, we often make it bigger than it ever was! Yikes! The sooner we can shift our focus back in the direction of something that feels *good*, the faster we get to feeling better and get back on track!

More about this in TOOL#4 below.

Remember why you've gone (or are going) to New School

Though it seems crazy that we would ever need extra encouragement to stay committed to doing the things we love that keep us happy, healthy and connected, often we do. When we have been in the habit of observing and then reacting to the world around us and the requests of other people asking us not to be selfish so we can do what *they* want us to do, it is easy to get off track. Sometimes some of that old school mentality will sneak in there and tell us we should be doing something else or working harder, which can also send us down a side street. The key to staying focused is keeping the passion and love alive and well!

More about this in TOOL#5 below.

Start by picking ONE thing as you move into New School & consciously work with The Power of FOCUS

A few of us who have experimented with taking on fifty new action steps at once (no comment! <lol!>), quickly discovered how the story ends. Instead of happily ever after, it's more like *stressed-out-right-back-at-square-one-and-mad-at-myself-after!* Not pretty!

Even though making only one change may seem like such a small step, if you truly commit to really focusing on one new Allowing Power Tool every thirty days, by the end of a year's time you will be amazed with how far you have come and what your life looks like! What's even better is your one thing may actually combine more than one thing, doubling, tripling or even quadrupling your efforts!

More about this in TOOL#3 below.

The Bottom Line on The Power of FOCUS & New School

When it all comes down to it, EVERY tool in this book is based upon using the power of FOCUS in one way or another. Deciding to enjoy the journey, to focus upon what lights you up, to listen to your inner guidance above all else and to act accordingly is THE most powerful step you can take to aligning with your dreams and visions. You Allow yourself to experience FREEDOM of the highest order that comes from knowing that no one and nothing ever need dictate how you feel ever again. You become an example of excellence and truly ARE in a position to be of service to humanity. The best part of all is that because you know what you know now, no matter where you may happen to be in relationship to Allowing Your Success, you ARE on your way, baby! Now that's what I call a focus on fabulousness!!

———

Only you control what it is you perceive or choose to turn the other cheek toward the answers that you seek – and let your freedom ring – focus is everything...

from "Focus is Everything"
© 2011 T.T.R.H.

The Power of FOCUS: Allowing Power Tools

Are you ready to start Allowing Your Success? Here are some New School tools you can use to harness the life-changing Power of FOCUS:

NOTE: Many Allowing Power Tools in this section and throughout this book involve writing. Why? Writing is a great FOCUS tool in and of itself and across the board. When we choose to take the time to write something down, we are at that moment focusing both mentally AND physically and are far less likely to be distracted!

Remember, for best results, focus on the tools that feel best to you now
(= give you a lighter feeling or sense of relief).

**TOOL#1
CHOOSE YOUR DESTINATION—
EVEN FOR SHORT TRIPS!**

By knowing where you are going and choosing what you want to experience before you set out on your journey, you set powerful wheels in motion for Allowing Your Success!

———————

DO THIS:

Every time you are preparing to take some kind of action or engage in an experience:

1. State out loud or put in writing the results you would like to experience/how you want to feel.

    •   Start by answering this question if you have not already done so:

    "What results would I like to experience while reading this book?"

---

2. Take an extra moment to picture/hear/feel what that result/ experience would be like.

3. Go forth and take action while you enjoy the journey!

   For a personal example of this tool in action visit:
   www.AllowingYourSuccess.com/SecretPages

   - ☛ Then use the code AYS-tjitd
   - ☛ Then choose ALLOWING Power Tools
   - ☛ Then The Power of FOCUS
   - ☛ Then TOOL#1: CHOOSE YOUR DESTINATION

TOOL#2
BUILD ON A SOLID FUNdation BY CREATING YOUR JOY LIST

JOY is THE key for lasting commitment!

DO THIS:

When you are wanting to stay in the driver's seat of your life and enjoy the journey!

1. Write out a list of all of the FUNdational things that you KNOW help you to stay in the flow of life and enjoy the journey.

As you read this book, you may even get some new ideas that feel good A side benefit from putting this list together—IT FEELS GOOD!!

> For a personal example of this tool in action visit:
> www.AllowingYourSuccess.com/SecretPages
>
>> ☛ Then use the code AYS-tjitd
>> ☛ Then choose ALLOWING Power Tools
>> ☛ Then The Power of FOCUS
>> ☛ Then TOOL#2: BUILD ON A SOLID FUNdation

TOOL#3
EXPERIENCE THE MAGIC OF ONE...

Pick ONE thing from your joy list and work it or "play it" for 30 days to multiply your results!

———◆———

DO THIS:

When you are wanting to stay in the flow of Allowing Your Success!

1. Pick ONE thing from your Joy List and play with using it consistently for 30 days.

   For a personal example of this tool in action visit:
   www.AllowingYourSuccess.com/SecretPages

   - ☛ Then use the code AYS-tjitd
   - ☛ Then choose ALLOWING Power Tools
   - ☛ Then The Power of FOCUS
   - ☛ Then TOOL#3: EXPERIENCE THE MAGIC OF ONE

TOOL#4
DO WHAT YOU LOVE OR FIND THE LOVE IN IT!

Wherever there is a focus on love and enjoying the journey, there is success!

———◆———

DO THIS:

When you'd like to experience better results with every action you take

1. Do what you love! (that's easy...) OR when you know in your gut that there are some not-so-fun things that (at least for now) are still a part of your personal equation for success, take the time to FIND the love FIRST.

   - Start by making a list (via pen and paper or type into your computer, iPhone/etc.) of your most important Things to Do.

   - Choose one item that you feel is the most important to do now.

   - Ask, "What are the positive aspects/what do I or can I love/ enjoy about doing this?" and keep going until you feel a marked emotional shift.

Feeling good? NOW you're ready to take action!!

For a personal example of this tool in action visit:
www.AllowingYourSuccess.com/SecretPages

   ☞ Then use the code AYS-tjitd
   ☞ Then choose ALLOWING Power Tools
   ☞ Then The Power of FOCUS
   ☞ Then TOOL#4: DO WHAT YOU LOVE

TOOL#5
KEEP THE NEW SCHOOL FIRE BURNING

Remember why you're doing what you do!

———◆———

DO THIS:

When you feel yourself needing a little help to stay focused

1. Write down or speak out loud to yourself why you've chosen to go to New School or why your chosen Joy List item is so awesomely awesome!

    For a personal example of this tool in action visit:
    www.AllowingYourSuccess.com/SecretPages

    - ☛ Then use the code AYS-tjitd
    - ☛ Then choose ALLOWING Power Tools
    - ☛ Then The Power of FOCUS
    - ☛ Then TOOL#5: KEEP THE NEW SCHOOL FIRE BURNING

TOOL#6
FOCUS FLIP

*Shift your focus to get back on the path of Allowing
your success!*

————◆————

DO THIS:

*When you need to shift your focus and get back to enjoying
the journey!*

1. Write it down: What I DON'T like/the problem and overall feeling.

2. Write it down: What I DO like/would like instead and overall feeling.

3. Write it down: Why I like (insert your answer to #2 "What I do like/want instead" here).

4. Write it down: What other area/areas of my life or life experiences DO feel like (insert your answer to #2 "What I do like/want instead" here).

For a personal example of this tool in action visit:
www.AllowingYourSuccess.com/SecretPages

- ☛ Then use the code AYS-tjitd
- ☛ Then choose ALLOWING Power Tools
- ☛ Then The Power of FOCUS
- ☛ Then TOOL#6: FOCUS FLIP

The Power of Words:
Focused Phonics

Want to enroll in New School and be fabulously focused?
Talking the talk will help you walk the walk...

Instead of Lazy Lingo	Use Focused Phonics
I never finish what I start and am such a procrastinator.	What I've chosen to change feels very doable and it feels good to do it now.
I'm always too tired to...	I've noticed that taking the time to do the things I love actually gives me MORE energy.
There's just not enough time for me to...	My time and my life are valuable, so I know it is wise to invest in the things that increase my experience of joy that are in alignment with what really matters to me.
I already have too much structure and too many responsibilities at work/home. The idea of adding something else feels crazy.	I can add one small thing that feels good and helps me to remember who I am because I deserve it for ME and THEY (my family, friends, clients, etc.) also deserve to experience the best of me.

The Power of Music for FOCUS

Download music for The Power of FOCUS
by visiting this link: www.AllowingYourSuccess.com/SecretPages

- ☛ Then use the code AYS-tjitd
- ☛ Then choose ALLOWING Music
- ☛ Then The Power of FOCUS
- ☛ Then, click on the song title of your choosing and ENJOY!

*Thank you in advance for honoring and respecting the value of our work and using this code just for you and your household.

Additional Resources for
The Power of FOCUS

Movies, Books & Beyond:

All *Star Wars* films

Jillian's Vantage (short film)

That's Magic (short film)

August Rush (film)

Make Believe
(film-a great comparison of Old School/New School)

Emmanuel's Gift* (film-documentary)

All and any books, audio books or DVDs by Abraham-Hicks

The Best Year of Your Life – Debbie Ford

The Power of Intention – Dr. Wayne Dyer

The Seven Spiritual Laws of Success – Deepak Chopra

Living Juicy – Sark

SoundsTrue.com (multiple titles, authors and resources)

Shambhala.com (multiple titles, authors and resources)

HayHouse.com (multiple titles, authors and resources)

Transformation-Publishing.com (multiple titles, authors and resources)

*Contains some not-so-pretty footage in places but this true story of a living human being is an astounding testimony of The Power of FOCUS.

To access our current list of ever-expanding resources visit:
http://AllowingYourSuccess.com/allowing_resources.php

<u>Your Journey So Far:</u>

FOCUS.

2. The Power of PRESENCE: Allowing Keys

NOW is when we ALLOW!

There's a reason why NOW rhymes with ALLOW

A great teacher once said "The present is the point of power." Even when we are thinking about our past or our future, we are doing it NOW. The journey IS the destination and the journey is happening right NOW. The present moment is our most precious gift and it is when and where Allowing happens—or not. Knowing this, it is clear to see that using your NOW wisely is THE determining factor in whether or not you Allow your success.

Presence and Intention— east meets west

As a student of life who has studied many religions, philosophies and spiritual paths of both east and west, I have come to discover a fundamental truth—that choosing our destination (whether for short trips or for the long term) and living/BEING in the NOW are both essential to Allowing success. It is no accident that I chose to begin this section of the book with The Power of FOCUS, immediately followed by The Power of PRESENCE, because once we set our destination, it is in the present moment that we:

- Align with and Alllow our intentions to come to us.

- Receive cues from our Source as to what to do next.

- See evidence of our intentions unfolding.

- Connect with our true timeless, infinite nature.

BEING in the NOW = no resistance = ALLOWING!

Another incentive for embracing moments of pure presence is that there is NO STRESS! When you are fully plugged into this magical moment, you are not thinking about the past or the future, nor are you judging, criticizing or resisting anything. You are simply being and BEING = ALLOWING!

Look at it this way: When we get too caught up in praying, planning or doing, we aren't able to see the signs or receive the answers, and create an ongoing cycle of perpetually *chasing* our dreams rather than *living* them. If you think about chasing, that usually occurs when something is running AWAY from us!

The wait is over: Where there is presence there is no need for patience!

The Power of...Patience?

Sometimes when we are looking to Allow something new into our lives and move beyond where we have been, there seems to be a degree of patience required. I've laughed out loud a few times when I've caught myself whining about one thing or another that "STILL hasn't changed yet, dammit!" because noticing it hasn't changed yet and then yapping about it is THE very thing that keeps it from happening!

The journey IS the destination and the Law of Attraction is always on the job, so when your NOW journey is all about waiting and impatience, guess what the destination is? More of the same!

Understandably, when you've had a certain pattern of thought (AKA belief) and an associated **REP** (Repeating Emotional Pattern) in place that has been years in the making, it often does take some time to align with your new-and-improved life. What is there for an "I want it and I want it now!"-type person to do when patience is just one big drag? Stop waiting and get back to enjoying the journey NOW!

Where there is presence, there is no need for patience!

Imagine never having to wait for anything ever again! This may seem improbable, but when you actively engage in our NOW by:

- appreciating what you DO have.

- quieting your mind and simply being.

- making feeling good or better your top priority and choosing thoughts and actions in the moment that are all about enjoying the journey.

...patience and waiting are no longer necessary!

By simply focusing on being or immersing yourself in the positive aspects of your now, you stop noticing and perpetuating the absence of something you want and start Allowing the PRESENCE of what you want!

Consciousness is KEY (Reprise)

Because you receive real-time emotional feedback telling you how close you are to your desired destination, the more conscious you are of what you are thinking and feeling at any given time, the more you stay at the helm of choosing thoughts that move you toward what you want while actively enjoying your now.

Instead of going mentally out to lunch and getting on a train of thought that takes you to a place you do NOT want to visit, you can make course adjustments the second you feel that slight bit of tension or experience a little dip in your energy. You can then consciously choose to get back on the track of feeling good immediately and reestablish your great connection and groovy vibe of Allowing!

Breathe to get off the train (of thought)

Even the most positive, happy people hop on a train to funkytown every now and again. Whether you choose to stop and breathe in and out one time or sit quietly for several minutes, slowing your breathing and focusing entirely on your breath is a great way to bring the train back to the station so you can actively choose a new, feel-good train (of thought)! In any case, even one second a day of presence is one more second of Allowing and therefore, worth celebrating! Is there any wonder why breathing is the most natural thing we do?

For some suggestions on conscious breathing techniques, see TOOL#1 below.

Get out of your mind by coming to your senses

The keys to presence are literally right under your nose, on the tip of your tongue, next to your ears, at your fingertips and right before your eyes! Choosing to use one of your sensational senses to bring you back to now is another great way to shift into neutral and even find your way back to your Allowing party!

More about this in TOOL#2 below.

Pump up the POP Factor (Power of PRESENCE) to stay on track with Allowing Your Success

Although the notion of multitasking may seem like the way to get more done, have you noticed that multitasking rarely leads to excellence or Allowing Your Success? Imagine how much more joy you could derive from feeling effective and efficient in EVERY act. That's when life REALLY POPS!! For example:

POP-work: Putting full attention on the task at hand = REALLY getting the job done and achieving better results!

POP-conversation: Truly listening to everyone you interact with and sharing what you feel in the moment rather than a predetermined thought = The gift of true respect and appreciation for others and authentic communication that Allows all parties to express themselves.

(On a business note, clients—like ALL human beings—REALLY appreciate feeling like their views and desires have been heard, which often results in winning their business!)

POP-cleaning: Noticing and appreciating the details of creating order = Fully enjoying every step of the transformation.

POP-exercise: Immersing yourself in the experience of moving your body = Moving through a full and natural range of motion (which typically means no boo-boos), feeling the strength of your body and placing more attention on what you CAN do.

POP-sex: Feeling every sensation completely = Heightened pleasure and a deep connection with your partner (Talk about enjoying the journey! Oh baby!)

The Bottom Line on The Power of PRESENCE

At the risk of being redundant (and saying it again any way <lol!>), NOW is when we ALLOW and live our unique version of the **BPI** (Big Picture Intention), which is all about having a fabulous NOW. Embracing a life of PRESENCE means that no matter where you may find yourself, you can always get back to being who you truly are and enjoy the journey right NOW or now or now...

There is no time limit.

There is no deadline.

There is no finish line, only a life-long adventure with LIFE ITSELF as the reward!

...and right now YOU SO Totally Rock!

"In the cathedral of my soul, in the temple of myself, I find everything I could possibly need, and all is well..."

from "Cathedral of My Soul"
© 2011-12 T.T.R.H.

The Power of PRESENCE: Allowing Power Tools

Here are a few surprisingly simple tools you can use to expand The Power of PRESENCE:

Remember, for best results, focus on the tools that feel best to you now
(= give you a lighter feeling or sense of relief).

TOOL#1
BREATHE TO GET OFF THE TRAIN (of thought)

Inhale to get a breath of fresh air!

DO THIS:

When you need to relax, release a thought, clear the air or get back in sync with your true nature

(Feel free to experiment to see which works best for you and try any of these with eyes open or closed. Closed is better whenever possible as it is easier to focus inward)

1. The Natural Slow-Mo:

    *   slow your natural breathing slightly on the first breath.

    *   slow down a little more on the next breath, then the next until you reach a comfortable, relaxed rhythm.

    *   every time you exhale, Allow your neck, shoulders, etc. to relax more and more.

2. The Dolphin Breath (great for releasing tension):

    *   breathe deeply into your diaphragm (belly area) for a slow count of 4-8 seconds.

- hold your breath for 4-8 seconds.

- puff out your cheeks a little then blow out strongly with an audible "puh," like a dolphin pushing air out of its blow hole.

- repeat as desired.

3. The Laughing Breath:

- take a nice, slow deep breath into your diaphragm.

- exhale while simulating "ha ha ha ha" (with or without sound).

- repeat as desired.

4. Four-Four-Four*:

- inhale slowly for 4 seconds into your diaphragm.

- hold your breath for 4 seconds.

- exhale for a count of 4.

- repeat as desired.

*Some find it natural to wait 4 seconds before inhaling again for an overall rhythm of 4-4-4-4. Try both to see what works best for you.

5. Simply stop, inhale, exhale and ask the question, "What if I just got back to being here now?"

If ever I catch myself on a funky train of thought or my mind starts wandering during focused quiet time, this simple question really helps to bring me back to the present moment.

6. Extended Presence Meditation:

When your goal is to sit quietly for several minutes, try these options for using breathing for meditation.

Based on the 4-4-4 breathing technique above:

- count 1, 2, 3, 4 in your mind as you inhale.

- count 1, 2, 3, 4 in your mind as you hold.

- count 1, 2, 3, 4 in your mind as you exhale.

- repeat as desired.

Based on the Natural Slow-Mo technique above:

- take a few breaths to get to a pace that feels good to you.

- take a deep breath in and as you exhale say (1) "Wuuuuuuuuuuuhhhhhhhhhhhnnnnnn."

- repeat, chanting the next number (2) "Toooooooo," then (3) "Threeeeeeeeeeee," etc. (if you prefer, you can certainly opt for using the "Ooooohhhmmm" sound or different vowel sounds - "Ahhhhhh," "Aaaaaayyyyy," "Eeeeeeeee," "Ooooooooo").

Feel and color your breath:

- whatever style of breathing you choose, really feel the breath as it moves from your throat, through your chest, down into your diaphragm, then as it moves back up and out.

- give it a color and "follow it" as it moves in and out of your body.

    If you are familiar with the Chakra system you can even use specific colors for relaxation, inspiration, and invigoration:

    Red: energizing, grounding

    Orange: invigorating, joyful

    Yellow: empowering, sunny outlook

Green: heart-opening, soothing

Sky Blue: clear communication, calming

Indigo: clarity of vision, insight

Violet: inspiration, Divine connection

...or simply visualize your favorite color or a color that makes you feel good.

Adding a sound, a vision, or a focused feeling to your breathing can be a great way to keep the mind singularly focused to open the door for some prime Allowing time!

TOOL#2
GET OUT OF YOUR MIND BY COMING TO YOUR SENSES

The keys to presence are literally right under your nose – and on the tip of your tongue, next to your ears, at your fingertips and right before your eyes!

———————

DO THIS:

Any time you need a little help getting back to now

1. Plug in to your senses – for example:

Vision: Zoom - Telescope/Microscope
Look around the room for something beautiful and really focus upon it or get up close and personal with an object to really examine its finer details.

Hearing: The Amplifier
Close your eyes and actively listen to the sounds in the room, noticing first the loudest, most prominent sound, then listen more closely for other less obvious sounds.

Touch: Pressure Points
Pet your cat/dog/squirrel, etc. or touch your bed sheets using varying degrees of pressure, really Allowing yourself to enjoy the sensations fully.

Smell: Stop and smell the roses—REALLY!
My hubby giggles at me every time we go out for a walk because I take "stop and smell the roses" in the most literal sense possible! If there are any sweet-smelling flowers, candles, incense, hot food or coffee in your vicinity, making a point of getting "nosey" is a great way to bring yourself right into your now.

Taste: The Connoisseur
Eating, drinking, and therefore activating our sense of taste, is SUCH a great way to experience presence since it also incorporates three

other senses: vision, touch and smell (and when eating crunchy foods, even our sense of hearing can participate, hitting five out of five!) Admire the beauty of how your food/drink is presented. Sip or chew slowly to really enjoy all of the flavors of what you are eating or drinking. Let yourself really feel the texture of the food or the liquid moving into your throat, then savor all of the wonderful smells associated with your dining experience.

A fun way to dine with Zen and even incorporate The Power of BEAUTY (more on this in Chapter 3, The Power of BEAUTY) is to treat EVERY meal or beverage like an expert foodie or wine tasting event. In this case, your goal is to state the facts and focus on appreciating what you are taking in. Get out a piece of paper or challenge a friend to play with you in describing every facet of what is on your plate or in your glass. Think: Presentation, dominant colors, textures, spices, aromas, notes, etc. If nothing else, discussing the bouquet of your tap water and how it pairs so nicely with your toast and butter with a friend could result in quite a few giggles! (Laughter by the way, is also a PHENOMENAL Allowing power tool! More about this is Chapter 10, The Power of HUMOR).

TOOL#3
FULL SYSTEM TUNE IN AND ZEN-TIME BED TIME

Waking up and going to sleep in Zen mode is a great way to start and end a day with Allowing!

———◆———

DO THIS:

To bring some calm and clarity into your waking life and help with restful sleep and sweet dreams

1. Rather than jumping into thoughts of what you have to do today, did yesterday or might do tomorrow, treat yourself to pleasant things to see, hear, taste, touch or smell:

Here are sample waking up/going to sleep routines:

*   listen to the sounds in the room or put on a fave CD.

*   focus on something beautiful in your room the moment you open your eyes (and just before turning out the lights at night).

*   feel the softness of the sheets, how nice it feels to pet your furry (feathered, scaled, etc.) friend or hug and kiss your human sweetheart.

*   breathe deeply to take in the smells in the room, the coffee that is ready in the kitchen in the morning (LOVE when that happens!) or the wonderful scent of incense as you prepare for sleep.

*   taste the fresh flavor of your toothpaste as you brush your teeth, or savor your night-time cup of tea.

TOOL#4
DISCOVER THE PRESENT IN EVERY ACTION AND
LET LIFE POP!

*Finding the **POP** Factor = enjoying the journey!*

————•————

DO THIS:

When you want to enjoy the journey more and be more effective
with whatever you are focusing on now

Simply focus on where you are and what you are doing fully, paying
close attention to detail. Let any thoughts that are not related to
what you are doing *right now* pass.

TOOL#5
FROM PATIENCE TO PRESENCE

Stop waiting and start living NOW!

DO THIS:

When you are waiting in line or are generally feeling impatient or restless and want to get back to enjoying the journey

1. Breathe to get off the train (of thought) – see TOOL#1 above.

2. To get out of your mind, come to your senses – see TOOL#2 above.

3. Revisit TOOL#6: FOCUS FLIP in the previous chapter, The Power of FOCUS.

The Power of Words:
ZENsational Conversation

Stating things in the present tense not only brings your focus back to the moment, it is also a great way to start training yourself to enjoy your intentions TODAY and NOW! Here are some samples of ZENsational Conversation.

Instead of Lazy Lingo	Use Focused Phonics
I've got so much to do today that eating or sleeping is a luxury I can't afford.	I know that I'll have what is required to accomplish the important stuff. Right now it feels good to be ___ (or doing) ___.
I wonder if this financial crisis will ever sort itself out. Times are SO tough for everyone.	I really love the idea of being the **CEO** of my life and knowing that I can choose to feel good now.
Man, it's taking FOREVER to get what I want!	I am Allowing the perfect timing and circumstances for what I want to show up and in the meantime, I am enjoying my NOW.
My mind is SO busy that I can't see how I'll ever feel anything close to Zen.	I have the power to focus and know that even one second of a quiet mind is another second I invest in Allowing my success!

The Power of Music
for PRESENCE

Download music for The Power of PRESENCE
by visiting this link: www.AllowingYourSuccess.com/SecretPages

- ☛ Then use the code AYS-tjitd
- ☛ Then choose ALLOWING Music
- ☛ Then The Power of PRESENCE
- ☛ Then click on the song title of your choosing and ENJOY!

*Thank you in advance for honoring and respecting the value of our work and using this code just for you and your household.

Additional Resources for
The Power of PRESENCE

Movies, Books & Beyond:

Peaceful Warrior, based on the novel by Dan Millman (film)

Forrest Gump (film)

Getting Into The Vortex, Book and Meditation CD
by Abraham-Hicks

The Power of Now and *A New Earth* by Eckhart Tolle

ZEN 24/7, by Phillip Toshio Sudo

Way of the Peaceful Warrior, by Dan Millman

8 Minute Meditation, by Victor Davich

Big Mind – Big Heart, by Dennis Genpo Merzel

Accelerated Meditation DVD—Part of the World Wealth 2008 series,
available through jamesray.com (phenomenal and transformational)

The Sedona Method – Sedona.com

SoundsTrue.com (multiple titles, authors and resources)

Shambhala.com (multiple titles, authors and resources)

HayHouse.com (multiple titles, authors and resources)

Transformation-Publishing.com (multiple titles, authors and resources)

Observe nature, your pet or young children.
They are all great "Zen Masters!"

To access our current list of ever-expanding resources visit:
http://AllowingYourSuccess.com/allowing_resources.php

Your Journey So Far:

FOCUS
on PRESENCE.

3. The Power of BEAUTY: Allowing Keys

Shift your focus to BEAUTY and watch your scenery change!

The Power of BEAUTY is a Divine way to Allow Success

"Beholding beauty with the eye of the mind, he will be enabled to bring forth, not images of beauty, but realities (for he has hold not of an image, but of a reality), and bringing forth and nourishing true virtue to become the friend of God and be immortal, if mortal man may..."

~Plato~

Isn't it amazing that when you are fully immersed in the experience of beauty, it is always an uplifting experience?

If you have ever lost yourself in a magnificent:

- **sight** - such as gazing upon a waterfall, red rocks or mountains, a mesmerizing photograph or painting, looking into your baby's eyes

- **sound** - like the pure tones of a chime, a magnificent piece of music, the laughter of someone you love or thunderous applause

- **smell** - orange blossoms in full bloom, fresh popcorn, your favorite cologne or perfume worn by your lover

- **taste** - insert favorite food/beverages here!

- **tactile experience** - feeling silk against your skin, a plush warm blanket, a nice soothing hot or refreshing cool shower

...you know firsthand what The Power of BEAUTY can do for you!

Beauty is our natural state of being

Perhaps it is because, as Keats would say, "Beauty is truth, truth beauty," there is a deep place within each of us that resonates with the essence of beauty.

Beauty IS our natural state of being, which is why it feels SOOO good to experience it. When we recognize the beauty in a thought, thing or experience, (therefore eliciting positive emotion), we see the world through the eyes of our Source. In so doing, we are in mac-daddy Allowing mode as we stretch out a big, fat red carpet for our intentions to saunter up to us in grand fashion!

Beauty is a place from which inspiration is born.

Beauty is an "E-Ticket" or "Fast-Pass" to a destination of joy.

Beauty has magnetic power to attract more of the same on multiple fronts and draw it forth from within.

Beauty is a gateway to The Power of PRESENCE.

Beauty is who we are and the true nature of all things.

As Forrest Gump might say, "beauty is as beauty does."

Invite The Power of BEAUTY by focusing on it throughout the day

Ever notice that the more you talk about or notice things, the more pronounced they become in your life?

Sometimes while in the middle of a major life change, spending time with people who can be challenging or driving through a run-down section of town, it is all too easy for your eyes and ears to focus on the shadows of life. In contrast, when you stop to Allow yourself to be more aware in these moments and make the decision to look for beauty, you break the spell of the shadows and start inviting and experiencing more and more light. As you remember, focus is everything, and NOW is when you Allow, so the more you focus on beauty, the more beauty becomes the nature of your now, your life, your experience and YOU!

Increasing your RDA of Beauty greatly contributes to staying in an Allowing flow

Beauty is music to the soul. Increasing your RDA (Recommended Daily Allowance) of beauty can greatly help your mind, body, spirit and level of productivity, as well as help you maintain or reconnect with an Allowing flow. Sometimes, when I have projects that require sitting at my computer keyboard for several hours, I take my laptop out on the porch. At night, I light candles, burn incense or put on some music to add some beauty to my work experience. Just as Mary Poppins said, *"Just a spoon full of sugar..."*

Allowing yourself to be in beautiful surroundings also gives you great material for future creations. Does having dinner at a 5-star restaurant sound like your idea of beautiful? Even if you go once a week or month just for dessert, coffee or a beverage of choice, you help to pave the way for that full dinner, just by getting your beautiful foot in the door!

Creating something beautiful is a 2-for-1 special!

In my own experience, I have discovered that writing songs or articulating ideas that increase beauty in the world greatly help me stay in a feel-good flow and reconnect with a sense of well-being when needed. Taking things a step further by sharing these creations and potentially inspiring a fellow traveler is a great 2-for-1 special, indeed! Creating and sharing the beautiful things, gifts, experiences or ideas YOU have within you truly IS the gift that keeps on giving!

The Bottom Line on The Power of BEAUTY

Experiencing and expressing beauty in the world is one of the greatest joys of being alive. The more you FOCUS on the PRESENCE of BEAUTY in your life, the more you attract and Allow your beautiful expanded reality and SELF. You fully enjoy the journey by recognizing that life truly is a work of art. By doing so, you become a light in the world and a shining example of just how beautiful Allowing success can be!

Welcome home, beautiful.

———

"...The power of beauty, profound and clear
My timeless yet familiar friend

She delivers me to my ever-present now

And brings me home again..."

from "The Power of Beauty"
© 2012 T.T.R.H.

ALLOWING Your Success!   The Power of BEAUTY

The Power of BEAUTY: Allowing Power Tools

Here are some Power Tools you can use to harness the awesome power of BEAUTY:

Remember, for best results, focus on the tools that feel best to you now
(= give you a lighter feeling or sense of relief).

TOOL#1
WAKE UP WITH BEAUTY

Want a beautiful day? Get a beautiful start!

———◆———

DO THIS:

When you want to consciously focus on beauty and attract/Allow more in your journey

1. Upon waking, set an intention to look for and focus on beauty throughout the day.

2. Keep or place an object, photograph, flowers/etc., that you consider to be beautiful close to your bedside and let that be the first thing you focus upon when you open your eyes to greet the day.

For example:

A huge oil painting with a big orange hibiscus and the words "Life is Beautiful" hangs right next to my side of the bed and almost always inspires a smile!

3. Wake up smiling!

Greeting your day (and your life) with a smile is another simple, but effective way to get going in the beautiful flow of Allowing Your Success!

TOOL#2
BEAUTIFUL INVITATION

Invite beauty by focusing on it throughout the day

———◆———

DO THIS:

When you want to stay in a feel-good flow and really emphasize the experience of beauty (see item 1 below)

When you want an extra beauty boost and you're having a tough time finding anything in your immediate environment to appreciate (see item 2 below)

When you want to shift your focus in a more pronounced way (see item 3 below)

1. Note every time you witness something beautiful (an object, a display of love and affection, a beautiful resolution, etc.).

    Make a clear mental note of it.

         or

    Make a statement of appreciation out loud.

         or

    Write it down/make note of it in a "Beautiful List."

The more evidence you have that there is always beauty to be found, the more you will continue to find!

2. Play the "Opposite Game."

Take a moment to ponder the opposite of what you are observing in your mind or put in it writing.

Examples:

Observing conflict? Think about how wonderful it is when you have experienced peace and cooperation.

Smell something really funky? Think about how much you appreciate the smell of something you really like.

Letting go of some kind of physical pain? Find another place in your body that feels good and give THAT your attention.

> For a personal example of this tool in action visit:
> www.AllowingYourSuccess.com/SecretPages
>
> - ☛ Then use the code AYS-tjitd
> - ☛ Then choose ALLOWING Power Tools
> - ☛ Then The Power of BEAUTY
> - ☛ Then TOOL#2 BEAUTIFUL INVITATION

3. Revisit TOOL#6: FOCUS FLIP in Chapter 1, The Power of FOCUS.

TOOL#3
SPEND TIME IN BEAUTIFUL PLACES

Beauty is music to the soul. Immerse yourself in beauty and feel your mood change!

DO THIS:

When you want to stay or get back into an Allowing flow

1. Go to a beautiful place you love and set a clear intention to be fully present while there and enjoy it to the max!

2. Beautify your space by adding things that delight your senses in beautiful ways.

TOOL#4
CREATE SOMETHING BEAUTIFUL

The action of creating beauty is something that can be therapeutic for anyone at any time and may even inspire someone else—a great 2-for-1 special!

DO THIS:

When you want to stay in an Allowing flow, align with more of a feeling of well-being, simply need a distraction or want to help inspire others

1. Create something beautiful! Here are some examples:

- take photographs of beautiful things or moments.
- paint, sketch, sculpt or build something beautiful.
- write or compose something that emphasizes a feeling or experience of beauty.
- wash and detail your car, motorcycle, boat, plane, RV, etc.
- clean, organize, paint or redesign your home or office to make your living or working environment look and feel more beautiful.
- plant beautiful flowers and plants in your garden.
- partake in random acts of kindness.
- smile at passersby and share sincere compliments.
- volunteer for a solution-oriented organization you believe in.
- organize a beautiful event.
- plan a beautiful vacation.

TOOL#5
GO TO SLEEP WITH BEAUTY AND HAVE
A GOOD NIGHT RE-CAP!

Recalling the beauty you experienced today makes for a great bedfellow!

———————◆———————

DO THIS:

When you want your last thoughts before sleeping to be good ones and get a jump-start on a beautiful morning

1. If your thoughts start wandering in not-so-beautiful directions prior to bedtime, take a moment to breathe to get off the train (TOOL#1 in The Power of PRESENCE) and instead consider all the beautiful things you witnessed and/or created today. You can even take it a step further by:

   • *reviewing your Beautiful List if you created one.*
   • *taking a moment to create a Beautiful List now.*

2. Once you've considered your beautiful moments and had your Good Night Re-Cap, engage The Power of PRESENCE by simply noticing and BEING with the beautiful sights, sounds, scents, etc. in your bedroom as you slow down your train of thought and prepare for sleep.

Sometimes when we've experienced really beautiful and exciting things throughout our day, it can actually rev us back up rather than help us chill, so I recommend going this route mainly if you were not already in "Zen Time Bed Time" (TOOL#3 in The Power of PRESENCE) relaxed mode.

I will say this: It is FAR better to take a little longer to fall asleep because we're happy and excited about life than it is to be kept up with a case of the bummers! In many cases I've noticed that even when I have had less sleep due to keeping myself up later feeling juiced about life, I found that I still would wake up feeling far more rested and alive than on occasions when I'd slept more hours after going to sleep with a head full of funkiness!

A beautiful mind and happy countenance is all about staying in the flow of Allowing success and, in my opinion, is welcome at ANY hour of the day!

The Power of Words:
Fairest of Them All

Your words can be a work of art in helping you to attract and Allow beauty into your life. The more you talk about the beauty that is within and around you, the more you think about it. The more you think about it, the more you FEEL it. The more you feel it, the more you Allow it! Quite a beautiful cycle, indeed!

Instead of Mud-Slinging with the ugly step-sister	Take the High Ground with the fairest of them all
Look at all those buildings! Concrete is taking over my town!	Look at that beautiful flower growing in between the cracks. What a wonderful symbol of nature always finding a way.
S/he takes me for granted and does ___, ___, and ___ that drives me nuts!	S/he DOES ___, ___ and ___ with love and I so enjoy seeing her/his beautiful smile.
Every time I turn on the news or pick up a paper it looks like things are getting worse!	It's nice to choose to watch or read something that highlights the good in the world. *OR* It's interesting to see that after some of the most tragic events in history, people come together to help each other through it. What a beautiful testament to the human spirit.
I am surrounded by sadness and pain and it seems like there's no way out.	Even in the midst of some of the toughest experiences of my life, some kind of blessing always emerged. I am open to finding the beauty in this situation.

The Power of Music
for BEAUTY

Download music for The Power of BEAUTY
by visiting this link: www.AllowingYourSuccess.com/SecretPages

- ☛ Then use the code AYS-tjitd
- ☛ Then choose ALLOWING Music
- ☛ Then The Power of BEAUTY
- ☛ Then click on the song title of your choosing and ENJOY!

*Thank you in advance for honoring and respecting the value of
our work and using this code just for you and your household.

Additional Resources for
The Power of BEAUTY

<u>Movies, Books & Beyond:</u>

Maryanne Goes to The Market (short film)

Avatar (film with stunning visual effects!)

Chocolat (film featuring beauty through chocolate!)

A Not So Still Life
(film-documentary about the amazing journey of artist Ginny Ruffner)

Opa! (film with beautiful footage of Greece)

Any book, film or music that highlights beauty in ANY form

SoundsTrue.com (multiple titles, authors and resources)

Shambhala.com (multiple titles, authors and resources)

HayHouse.com (multiple titles, authors and resources)

Transformation-Publishing.com
(multiple titles, authors and resources)

PeterLik.com (astoundingly beautiful photography)

Andre Desjardins ("visual emotion-ism,"
the Da Vinci or Michelangelo of our time—wow!)

SigridTidmore.com (images to awaken the mind)

Roy Vance: yessy.com/roysart
(beautiful modern art paired with positive intentions)

Afsaneh's Art: ChangeThrivers.com
(hand painted, hand-picked, one-of-a-kind snail shells)

To access our current list of ever-expanding resources visit:
http://AllowingYourSuccess.com/allowing_resources.php

<u>Your Journey So Far:</u>

FOCUS
on the PRESENCE
of BEAUTY.

4. The Power of NATURE: Allowing Keys

Allowing Your Success is part of human-NATURE!

The Power of NATURE can shift your perspective back to Allowing Success

Looking for guidance? Want an attitude adjustment? Few things are as potent as The Power of NATURE to put things in perspective and give us the breath of fresh air we all need to stay balanced, clear and productive, and in an Allowing flow.

Virtually any time I have ever needed a time out or an extra dose of inspiration, I've noticed that sitting by some body of water, taking a hike in the woods, gazing at the stars at night, strolling through a beautiful garden or simply watching animals be and go about their lives has more than fit the bill.

One day, when I was feeling particularly stressed, I found myself sitting outside at a local restaurant surrounded by lots of noise – the last thing I needed at the time! Rather than continue to engage in the cacophony in my head and around me, I decided to fix my attention on the trees and clouds. After what seemed like only a minute or two, this simple act actually helped me to feel quiet and peaceful inside, despite the urban soundtrack, and reminded me of the plethora of gifts that await us when we remember to step outside the box and back into the circle of life.

Nature's inhabitants are master Allowers

Another huge bonus of tapping in to The Power of NATURE is that plants, animals, rocks, mountains, oceans, trees, the sky, the soil and everything in the natural world are master Allowers. I'm amazed when I watch my feline Zen Masters, Magic and Music—it is so easy for them to sleep ANYWHERE in the craziest positions! If they get into a frenzy playing and accidentally fall or bump into something, they never stop to whine or complain, they just get right back up as if nothing happened. A great example of Allowing indeed!

Having the great fortune of growing up with an American Indian brother also instilled within me a deep love and sense of reverence for Mother

Earth and her many inhabitants. This led me to study what is referred to as "animal wisdom"—how animals can be great teachers and guides in our day to day lives. After experiencing more amazing and timely encounters with all sorts of animals, birds and wildlife than I could possible recount, I have come to greatly value and welcome the appearance of the fascinating creatures that share our planet. For me, The Power of NATURE is a multi-platform medium for Allowing, and the gifts our great Mother has to offer can certainly be a gateway to peace, clarity, joy and Divine connection for any and all who are willing to stop, look and listen. For example:

Seeing lots of squirrels? Notice a hawk, woodpecker or unusual bird? Ladybugs, butterflies, grasshoppers or dragonflies seem to be following you? Pay attention to the animals (and even insects, trees and plants) that:

- keep showing up on a regular basis.

- make three appearances in a short period of time.

- do something to really grab your attention
  (especially animals, etc. you don't normally see).

When they do show up, think about what you would associate with the personality, color or behavior of that animal, for example:

Butterfly = colorful, the result of metamorphosis, free-flying.

Possible Translation: Allow more by looking for the beauty in all things; change can be magnificent; go with the flow of life...

Dolphin = playful, strong, breathe through a blow-hole, amplify their messages through water.

Possible Translation: Allow yourself to enjoy life more, remember to come up for fresh air, get in touch with your emotions and Allow creativity to flow...

Mockingbird = always singing, courageous, multi-lingual.

Possible Translation: Allow yourself to express your own unique voice, stand your ground, pay attention to communication...

Rabbit = take leaps and bounds or remain perfectly still, multiplicity, burrows have two "doors."

Possible Translation: Allow flexibility, gather your energy during quiet times so you are ready for the next big leap, abundance is imminent, always know there is more than one way to go forward...

A little more about human-NATURE

Just as with anything else "outside" of ourselves, remember that the wisdom from animals and nature in general is simply another guide to help you along your path and should never take the place of your inner guidance and direct connection with your Source. Yes, they ARE master Allowers and serve as great reminders to get back into the flow of life, but part of the fun of being human is our ability to sort through contrast in more pronounced ways in order to then create and Allow something new into our lives while enjoying the journey toward it. This is a little different from how our animal friends roll.*

My advice to you? As long as what you feel and receive from natural and animal wisdom feels good and adds joy to your life, roll with it! If, however, you ever feel like you have to see ten squirrels climbing a single tree, all moving in unison and singing the happy squirrel song before you Allow yourself to get in to your car to go about your day, it may be time to shift your focus!

*Due to living and being in such close proximity to us, sometimes domesticated animals can begin to take on more human characteristics and develop patterns of resistance. The best way to encourage your animal friend's natural Allowing tendencies? Give them more of your love and less of your worrying.

Nature reminds us to take a breath of fresh air

There is nothing more natural than breathing, and though we have this wonderful autonomic system in our bodies that keeps this process going without conscious focus, connecting with the nature of existence through conscious breathing is also a very real way to participate in the movement of what sustains us.

We could actually live for a while without food or water, but being able to breathe is non-negotiable! When we resist our flow of life and take shorter, shallower breaths, we literally cut off our own life force. It's no wonder when we feel overwhelmed that we ask for room to breathe and sometimes even physically manifest congestion or breathing difficulties. The solution? Let nature be your guide in reminding you to take a moment or two to breathe, to get off the funky train (of thought) and back IN to your natural state of Allowing.

Stop right now and take a slow, deep breath and feel it as it fills your body. Hold it for 4-5 seconds, then exhale slowly.

What happened to your muscles? Shoulders? Neck?

To remind yourself of some great breathing tools and techniques, revisit the Allowing Power Tools section of Chapter 2, The Power of PRESENCE.

The Bottom Line on The Power of NATURE

If we look at all the great masters throughout history, EVERY one of them knew, used, and respected the awesome Power of NATURE, incorporating her many gifts into their teachings and stories. So perhaps recognizing that The Power of NATURE can:

- help us plug into the infinite wisdom that surrounds us.

- lead us back to who we truly are.

- encourage us to follow the guidance that comes naturally from within.

- be an incredible tool for getting back to and staying in a natural flow of Allowing our Success.

and IS indeed human-NATURE after all!

Happy trails!

—•—

"...I open up my wings and I sail on by,
that's why I follow the butterfly..."

from "Follow The Butterfly"
© 2012 T.T.R.H.

The Power of NATURE: Allowing Power Tools

Here are some Power Tools you can use to harness the tremendous Allowing Power of NATURE:

Remember, for best results, focus on the tools that feel best to you now
(= give you a lighter feeling or sense of relief).

TOOL#1
GET OUT(SIDE) AND WATCH THE BEST SHOW ON EARTH!

Even five minutes outdoors can create a powerful shift in your perspective!

DO THIS:

When you need a breath of fresh air or want to stay in an Allowing flow

1. Take a few minutes to get outside anywhere you can.

2. Focus on a specific tree, plant, animal, cloud, etc. Simply observe and BE in the moment.

3. Before heading back indoors, make a mental note of or write down any particular sight, sound or insight that inspires or speaks to you.

TOOL#2
LOOK FOR ANIMALS HOLDING SIGNS

No, it won't be anything like, "Will work for shoes." BUT when animals show up consistently, they usually have a message for you that relates to Allowing or may even let you know your intentions are on the way!

———◆———

DO THIS:

When you are wanting guidance of some kind, insight on your Allowing style, to feel connected to Mother Earth or just for the fun of it!

1. Make a note/list of animals:

    • that you naturally like or are drawn to.

    or

    • keep a daily/weekly journal of animals:

        • that seem to be showing up consistently and are most prevalent in your life right now.

        • that are unusual or show up in odd places/ circumstances that really get your attention.

        • that show up at least three times in a day or week.

2. Next to each animal write down:

    • the characteristics you associate with the personality, color or behavior of that animal.

    • how you felt when you saw or thought about that animal, or the feeling you would associate with the animal.

3. Find out more about your animal (if you are inspired to do so) via the web or check out books about animal wisdom.

There are many great books about animal wisdom, also referred to as animal medicine, totems, spirit guides, etc., but what matters most is always what that animal or experience with nature means to YOU and how YOU feel when you see it.

For example:

When I see a cardinal, it is a reminder to trust. This may not be the typical message associated with cardinals, but it is one of the personal meanings I have come to associate with my red-crested friend.

Here's another example:

Once when I was missing my little feline friend, Lucky, who had just transitioned, I made the statement, "I really want to feel some comfort and peace." Literally seconds after stating my desire, my husband called me to come and see something right away.

I was startled to discover that a mamma raccoon had decided to bring her new babies up onto the roof right next to our bathroom window! She even put her nose and paws up against our window when I came over. Then, she trusted the situation enough to go get food, leaving her babies alone—for three days!

It was an extraordinary experience that still blows my mind to this day. So, in addition to the many keynotes associated with raccoons, I see them as a greeting from Lucky and a wonderful reminder that all is well. Interestingly enough, she had two babies with her and later that year I became the mommy of two new feline babies as well, Magic and a few months later, Music!

TOOL#3
KEEP BREATHING!

Our breath is our life force and can be used in a variety of ways for Allowing

---

DO THIS:

When you want to stay alive <lol!>, slow down, clear the air and get back to an Allowing flow

1. Stop right now and take a slow, deep breath and feel it as it fills your body. Hold it for 4-5 seconds, then exhale slowly.

2. Repeat as needed!

For more conscious breathing techniques, revisit TOOL#1 in Chapter 2, The Power of PRESENCE.

The Power of Words:
Natural Vernacular

HUH?? What does The Power of Words have to do with nature and animals? Experiment with Grid-Lock Lingo and Natural Vernacular and see for yourself...

Instead of Grid-Lock Lingo	Use Natural Vernacular
Everything (one) is in my way!	**WATER:** I go with the flow and always find a way.
That's SO wrong! S/he should...	**ALL ANIMALS:** What do I want right now?
I've got to beat the competition!	**TREES:** I grow and expand in my own unique way at the perfect rate for me by following the light. **OR** **STARS:** I create my own light and let it shine!
I am stuck in this situation and there is nothing I can do.	**BIRDS:** I can always rise above and discover another way.

The Power of Music
for NATURE

Download music for The Power of NATURE
by visiting this link: www.AllowingYourSuccess.com/SecretPages

- ☛ Then use the code "AYS-tjitd"
- ☛ Then choose ALLOWING Music
- ☛ Then The Power of NATURE
- ☛ Then click on the song title of your choosing and ENJOY!

*Thank you in advance for honoring and respecting the value of our work
and using this code just for you and your household.

Additional Resources for
The Power of NATURE

Movies, Books & Beyond:

The Emerald Forest (film)

Avatar (film)

Brother Bear (film)

Animal Speak by Ted Andrews

Power Animals by Steven D. Farmer

SoundsTrue.com (multiple titles, authors and resources)

Shambhala.com (multiple titles, authors and resources)

HayHouse.com (multiple titles, authors and resources)

Transformation-Publishing.com
(multiple titles, authors and resources)

Get OUT and watch the best show on earth:
Go for a hike, paddle, stroll or climb in a beautiful natural place near you!

Visit county, state and national parks

**To access our current list of ever-expanding resources visit:
http://AllowingYourSuccess.com/allowing_resources.php**

<u>Your Journey So Far:</u>

FOCUS
on the PRESENCE
of the BEAUTY
of your true NATURE.

5. The Power of APPRECIATION: Allowing Keys

Appreciation always leads to a great destination!

Appreciation defined

Appreciation, noun: an increase in price or value; understanding of the nature or meaning or quality or magnitude of something; an expression of gratitude.

Gratitude, noun: a feeling of thankfulness and appreciation.

Oooh, Gratitude! Ahhh, Appreciation! These are words I have easily come to love, as they have been those best friends that virtually always have a way to help me feel amazing.

There was one particular time in my life when I was navigating through some pretty rough waters *(while paddling upstream—not very smart!)* and was at a loss for what to do to get back to my normal smooth ride. After a few minutes of essentially giving up trying to figure things out, I suddenly felt an urge to write a list of ANYTHING positive I could find that could help me to feel even the slightest bit better. I started with small, simple stuff like "my windows catching the rays of sunlight," then "there's food in my fridge and love in my life..." and before I knew it this list took on a life of its own. By the time I had completed my list, a melody also took shape in my head in the form of a song called "I'm All Right"! Talk about changing my tune!

Considering where I had been just a few minutes earlier, I was astounded by how much better I felt in such a short period of time. Although we are all in different emotional places at different times, considering thoughts and then riding the wave of sincere appreciation is truly an auspicious way to move up the scale into the positive side of your equation (PLUS clear the runway for your intentions to show up ahead of schedule!)

Why is appreciation so powerful? When you are hanging out in the neighborhood of true appreciation, you activate The Power of BEAUTY and actually start seeing the world through the eyes of Source, AKA love. Love, by the way, is ROCKET FUEL for Allowing, folks!

The logic of Appreciation—meet Bob & Un-Bob

Even if this love talk is a little too flower-power-ish for you, let me paint a picture of how logical appreciation can be as an Allowing tool...

Promotion Time!! Bob's Story:

Bob started working in an entry level position with his company in the mail room, but has already identified that increased prosperity and the opportunity to do even more of what he loves is where he wants to be. Rather than lament his entry level position, Bob is thrilled that he has a way to feed his family, that he gets to work in a nice, air-conditioned office and is able move around all day. He takes pride in paying careful attention to whatever he is doing in the moment and if an important package comes in for one of the staff members, he will even go out of his way to hand-deliver it to its recipient. Bob is always a joy to be around, loves sharing sincere compliments and always has a smile for everyone who crosses his path. Bob simply radiates appreciation.

Promotion Time?? Un-Bob's Story:

Un-Bob also started working in the mail room and, like Bob, would love to move up the food chain. Un-Bob, however, wakes up every day at the last possible second, starts complaining about everything the moment he walks in the door, does the bare minimum, often places mail in the wrong boxes because his mind is virtually always elsewhere (he just wants to get it done and over with) and spends most of his time obsessing over when his big break is going to come because he just can't stand one more minute of "working in this dump!"

Who do you think is most likely to get promoted? Yep, Bob is our man! It's true that Bob is super nice and likable, but there are many nice people who stay in the mail room jobs of life. Bob made the leap because he:

- identified a clear and strong desire and knows where he's heading (like Un-Bob).

- found the joy in all he does by focusing on the positive aspects of his job (unlike Un-Bob).

- gave 100% of his attention to even the smallest tasks and did an impeccable job (Un-Bob, not so much!).

- felt sincere appreciation for where he is NOW (bummer, Un-Bob!).

The Bottom Line on Bob

When you think and feel like Bob, embodying a spirit of appreciation for both where you are and where you're going, only then are you are truly ready for more. On top of readying yourself for that next life promotion, you get the very real bonus of enjoying the journey and feeling good right NOW (oh darn!) instead of waiting until later (which never comes anyway)! Who knew that successful self-promotion is actually a game of sincere appreciation? You GO with your Bob-self!

Accentuate Appreciation

Though gratitude and appreciation are very closely related, be sure to keep your focus on the *appreciation* side of the equation.

Believe it or not, sometimes gratitude can dip down into the opposite side of the coin like "Thank goodness I don't have THAT to deal with!" placing our attention on the THAT that we do NOT want. It can also call forth a feeling of being in debt to someone or something which can also bring a bit of unwanted baggage along for the ride. I know it may seem like I'm splitting hairs here, but if you want to keep moving in the direction of what you DO want, focusing on APPRECIATION of the GOOD is where it's at! This is why I chose The Power of APPRECIATION* as the title of this section!

*If the word GRATITUDE is a word that resonates more with you, no worries! As long as you are focused on the feeling of appreciation, feel free to use the word that rocks YOUR world most.

Start early & stay late

Starting and ending your day with a focused practice of appreciation and tag of "thank you" is yet another fabulous way to stay in an Allowing flow. You consciously honor your Source AND yourself for choosing to feel good, which results in another magnificent 2-for-1 special; you get your day rolling on the fast track with Allowing and close up shop with a happy heart. Just like Bob, starting early and staying late is a great way to enjoy the journey AND get promoted, thereby Allowing Your Success!

See TOOL#1 below.

Put it in writing

Although simply pausing to consider thoughts of appreciation is indeed powerful, putting them in writing can greatly hone your point of focus, intensify your experience of positive feelings and give you the bonus of having some great material to draw from in the future if ever you need a little extra boost. Whether you keep an appreciation journal, update an appreciation blog or e-mail your appreciation to a friend, dedicating focused time to thoughts that feel good always produces feel-good results.

Sharing words of appreciation with others is also a two-way street that endows all involved parties with a barrage of feel-good material. Something I very much enjoy doing is sending unexpected greeting cards through the mail to family and friends, since articulating my appreciation for them really makes ME feel amazing!

More about this in the TOOL#2 below.

Thanks for the memories—thanks in advance!

As important as it is to live in the present moment, we humans tend to consider the past or the future quite a bit, often hanging out there more than we do HERE. The good news is there is absolutely nothing wrong or bad about mentally time traveling, but if you're going to do it, why not dig up the GOOD stuff rather than the growling dinosaurs or the grim reaper?!

When taking a trip down memory lane, make a mental or actual note of all of the past blessings you appreciate. I call this "Allowing Evidence." Reminding yourself that good things CAN and DO happen to you is a great way to build your belief that your new desires are also possible, which cranks up your Allowing factor BIG time.

When zooming ahead to the future, keep your focus on seeing your life as you really want it to be *(more on this in Chapter 7, The Power of OWNERSHIP)*. While you ponder living your intentions, add some extra juice to your Allowing power by saying "thank you" in your mind or out loud (or as Bob Proctor suggested in the movie/book The Secret, "I am so happy and grateful now that..."). When you say "thank you" in advance, you set the wheels in motion for welcoming your intentions because you align with the idea that they are already a done deal. The more done they truly feel, the faster they come, baby! Let the appreciation fiesta begin!

More about this in the TOOL#3 below.

Thanks for YOU!

Think about how good it feels when someone else showers YOU with appreciation and love. It totally rocks, no doubt! Because YOU are an amazing and most divine work of art, why not take a moment to give this gift to your SELF? YOU are responsible for making the choice to feel good at any given time, exercising your power of FOCUS. YOU are Allowing the floodgates of fabulousness to open, so you deserve some props! Besides, being nice to the **CEO** (AKA YOU!) is always a smart move!!

More about this in TOOL#4 below.

The Bottom Line on The Power of APPRECIATION: It's ALL good!

When you recognize that EVERYTHING in your world is helping you become a better and better Allower, it's ALL good! Even things that may appear to be bad, whether they are happening to you personally or are things you're observing in another person's experience, are simply an invitation to move toward something good in the long run! Contrast in simply an invitation for you to:

- clarify what you DO want.

- take a different road that could actually become a shortcut to your joy destination.

- be a shining example for others who are having difficulty seeing that there IS another way of being.

- see the shadows of life for what they really are—a way to get really good at shifting your thoughts so that no matter what goes on around you, you have the ability to feel good, hence becoming an ever-expanding master Allower of a truly magical life!

By embracing a spirit of true appreciation for EVERYTHING that crosses your path, you begin to experience a level of power, peace and joy that every truly great journey (and destination!) is made of!

I SOOOOO appreciate YOU!

———

"...Everything is conspiring to make this good life great,
so I appreciate..."

from "I Appreciate"
© 2011-12 T.T.R.H.

The Power of APPRECIATION:
Allowing Power Tools

Here are some Power Tools you can use to tap into the
AWESOME AWESOMENESS OF AHHH-PRECIATION:

Remember, for best results, focus on the tools that feel best to you now
(= give you a lighter feeling or sense of relief).

TOOL#1
START EARLY, STAY LATE

Want a great waking and resting experience? Tune in to appreciation/
gratitude!

DO THIS:

When you want to add even more Allowing Mojo to your waking up/
bedtime practice.

1. When engaging in your waking up/bedtime practice (as
    suggested in the chapters The Power of PRESENCE and The
    Power of BEAUTY), simply add the words "Thank you." For
    example:

"Thank you for <u>what I am doing/feeling/observing.</u>"

"Thank you for <u>all the cool stuff that I experienced today.</u>"

TOOL#2
PUT IT IN WRITING

Putting appreciation down in ink (or cyberspace) makes Allowing official!

———◆———

DO THIS:

Any time you want to Allow success, elicit more and more good from your life, relationships and the world at large, and shift your mood to a groovy-er place, dude!

1. Invest a few minutes each day in writing down (through whatever means or medium works best for you) what you appreciate NOW, truly focusing on the good and positive things in your life.

Doing this at the start or finish of your day is a great time, but "AHHHpreciation" feels like a breath of fresh air and rocks ANY time!

2. If you choose to do so and it feels good to you, share your daily list and the good vibrations with a loved one/friend or group of friends you love and trust (especially if you are acknowledging someone you love).

You can also invite them to participate in a daily practice of AHHHpreciation with you for the benefit of all!

A few close friends and I share our daily AHHHpreciation lists with one another via e-mail and often when I get to read what made the list for them, it either kicks my vibe up even higher or gives me a little extra boost of inspiration when I need it! I also dedicate a large percentage of my Blog to sharing AHHHpreciation, so visit http://AllowingYourSuccess.com/blog/ for real-time samples of appreciation in action.

TOOL#3
THANKS FOR THE MEMORIES, THANKS IN ADVANCE

If you're going to time travel, dig up the GOOD stuff!

---◆---

DO THIS:

When you want to stay or shift into a flow of GOOD Mojo when thinking about your past or future

1. Make a note of your Allowing Evidence.

If your mind starts wandering to the past, take a moment to consider a happy experience, or revisit one of your own stories of Allowing success that was all about going with the flow and enjoying the journey.

Kick things up a notch by putting your happy memory or Allowing story in writing or cyberspace and revisit any time you need a feel-good boost or want to add fuel to your belief that Allowing Your Success via enjoying the journey CAN happen for you (because it HAS!).

NOTE: *Pay attention to how you feel as you do this. If it activates any yucky feelings of "the past was better than now...," go back to appreciating the good in your present by playing with TOOL#2 above or revisit the Power Tools in Chapter 2, The Power of PRESENCE or Chapter 3, The Power of BEAUTY.*

2. Give thanks in advance.

Zoom ahead to Chapter 7, The Power of OWNERSHIP, TOOL#1, option 2: BUILDING THE NEW **CEO**, and TOOL#2: THE WHOLE PIE and simply add a tag of "thank you" at the start or end of completing these exercises.

TOOL#4
THANKS FOR YOU!

It feels SOOO good to give credit where credit is due!

———◆———

DO THIS:

*When you know the **CEO** (AKA YOU!) can use a little extra love*

1. Every time you catch yourself in the act of thinking, speaking or acting in a way that feels good, thank yourself by name either out loud or in your mind.

2. Look in the mirror as you appreciate YOU.

Just as others really dig it when words of love and appreciation are delivered with direct eye contact, your heart of hearts certainly appreciates receiving the same gesture!

If you feel any resistance to thanking yourself by name, simply thank God/Universe/Intelligence/Source because YOU are also the eyes and ears of the Infinite.

3. Put it in writing.

Write down these questions and answer them as if you were giving this list to a friend you deeply love who you'd like to appreciate and inspire:

*   what do I like about <u>my name here?</u>

*   what do I love about <u>my name here?</u>

*   what can I appreciate about <u>my name here?</u>

For a personal example of this tool in action visit:
www.AllowingYourSuccess.com/SecretPages

- ☛ Then use the code AYS-tjitd
- ☛ Then choose ALLOWING Power Tools
- ☛ Then The Power of APPRECIATION
- ☛ Then TOOL#4: THANKS FOR YOU!

TOOL#5
THE APPRECIATION TAG

Creating a tag as a reminder to embrace an attitude of appreciation can be a fun and powerful way to stay on the path of Allowing

———◆———

DO THIS:

When you want a little help remembering to focus on appreciation

1. Designate a song, color, symbol, shape, scent, picture, object (such as the gratitude rock in the movie The Secret), or even a time (such as 3 PM every day) as an appreciation tag.

2. Every time you come across your tag, use this as a cue to stop for a moment to plug into a few thoughts of appreciation.

Whatever tag you choose, let it be something you like, as this also ensures that even in the seeming absence of positive stuff in your immediate environment, your tag can in and of itself BE your point of appreciation!

3. Invite a few.

If you have a few friends, family members, or co-workers who would also enjoy expanding their experience of Allowing, choose a group tag (for work-mates, something associated with the company logo could be a nice choice). Any time you encounter the tag, each of you pause for a moment of appreciation.

This is a great way to bond with family and friends and encourage team spirit and high morale in the workplace!

The Power of Words:
Awesome Appreciation

*Speaking the lingo of appreciation is an incredible gift
to give yourself and all those around you.
Try it out and feel it for yourself!*

Instead of Copious Complaints	Use Awesome Appreciation
How can I appreciate when I have so much pain?!	I appreciate that my <u>insert well body part here</u> DOES feel good.
The service was SO terrible, blah, blah blah...	This experience really makes me appreciate how much I enjoy warm, friendly, helpful people.
I can't believe my stuff STILL hasn't shown up yet!	It's nice to remember that I HAVE received things I wanted in the past and it's always extra-cool when the timing works out perfectly for me to REALLY get to enjoy my stuff to the FULLEST!
Why is it so hard to...	I really appreciate how I just recognized that I was in a state of resistance and can choose to let go in this moment.

The Power of Music for APPRECIATION

Download music for The Power of APPRECIATION
by visiting this link: www.AllowingYourSuccess.com/SecretPages

- ☞ Then use the code AYS-tjitd
- ☞ Then choose ALLOWING Music
- ☞ Then The Power of APPRECIATION
- ☞ Then click on the song title of your choosing and ENJOY!

*Thank you in advance for honoring and respecting the value of our work
and using this code just for you and your household.

Additional Resources for
The Power of APPRECIATION

Movies, Books & Beyond:

Charlie and The Chocolate Factory (film)

Delivering Milo (film)

Beauty and the Beast (film)

The Man Who Never Cried (short film)

That's Magic (short film)

Gratitude (short film)

SoundsTrue.com (multiple titles, authors and resources)

Shambhala.com (multiple titles, authors and resources)

HayHouse.com (multiple titles, authors and resources)

Transformation-Publishing.com (multiple titles, authors and resources)

Share Appreciation! Visit www.SendOutCards.com
A great online greeting card company that I like to use that makes
sharing appreciation convenient, easy and fun

Watch a baby or young child smile, laugh and fully engage
with some fascinating toy, object or food item! Talk about appreciation!

To access our current list of ever-expanding resources visit:
http://AllowingYourSuccess.com/allowing_resources.php

Your Journey So Far:

FOCUS
on the PRESENCE
of the BEAUTY
of your true NATURE
with APPRECIATION.

6. The Power of AUTHENTICITY: Allowing Keys

When we think, speak and act from a place of AUTHENTICITY, Energy GROWS and Life FLOWS!

Authenticity and the BPI

Because living an authentic life is THE most natural impulse you can experience, the power of AUTHENTICITY is one of your most powerful Allowing Power Tools. In comparison to the immense amount of energy it *takes* to be, do or act in a way that we think others would most approve of, or behave based on what we think we should do, letting your true joyful nature and desires flow freely *gives* energy (among MANY other gifts) to your life. How do I know this? The same way you do! When I am experiencing something that fills me with joy to the core of my being:

- I feel like I can keep going and going and do whatever I am doing with love and precision, making it easy to commit to The Power of FOCUS.

- I am fully in my now, experiencing The Power of PRESENCE.

- I am living The Power of BEAUTY.

- I am mirroring the natural world and The Power of NATURE.

- I am fully aligned with The Power of APPRECIATION.

The Power of AUTHENTICITY rolls all five primary Allowing Power Tools into ONE! When you commit to doing what you love, it is easy to keep doing it. When you are in a state of joy, you are completely living in the moment. When you are in love with the moment, you radiate beauty. When you follow your bliss, you tap into the heart of Mother Earth herself. When you are blissful, you are appreciating...

...and when you are appreciating and feeling good, you Allow. It really is as simple as that! Living an authentic life (AKA doing what feels good) IS synonymous with living the **BPI** and Allowing success.

Enjoying the journey is synonymous with Authenticity and Allowing Success!

During the course of my life I have noticed an interesting phenomenon: Anytime I had to struggle and fight for something, my moment of glory was either extremely short lived or non-existent, and the climb up the next mountain was ten times harder! On the other hand, when I found myself "in the zone" and was really enjoying whatever I was doing, I felt good throughout the process AND—almost as if by magic—amazing things showed up for me (like my soul mate, money and opportunities popping up out of nowhere and even the idea for creating this book!) Imagine what you could Allow into your life by living joyfully and authentically?

Fulfilling the BPI is at the HEART of all authentic desires

One of the first important points to remember is the more truly authentic—AKA in alignment with the **BPI**—your desire is, the more likely you are to Allow it. How can you tell? It's elementary my dear Watson! If it feels great when you think about it, birds start singing your favorite song, the seas part and you notice your feet are now hovering three feet above the ground, it's a sure bet you ARE at this moment fulfilling the **BPI** and whatever you are focusing on is also part of your path of fabulousness!

It's also important to keep an open mind and really do your best to get to the heart of what it is you REALLY want. Sometimes the things or experiences you ask for are more about the how than the actual destination. THE destination for having or experiencing anything you think you want is always in essence the same for every living, breathing thing: You want it because you think you will feel better when you have it. Want more money? Want a soul mate? Want great health? Want an ultra-chic pad? Want a limited edition Bentley? It's all the SAME destination, folks. Get your stuff, feel good! It's no wonder that if all of your goodies are about feeling good, it makes sense that feeling good NOW is STILL the shortest path to the Emerald City!

As Dorothy said, "There's no place like home," so if you want your dreams and visions to materialize and let the Law of Attraction be your BFF, the best place to start is truly in your own back yard!

Following the flow of INSPIRED action can net far more than required action

If I get an idea to do something that feels good, I'm always open to give it a go because more often than not, I end up stumbling across the very person or thing I was looking for AND even some mind-blowing surprises! A bonus is the more you follow the feel-good call of inspiration, the less there is a need to act out of obligation.

Action with Authenticity: Meet the Chefs

Doing anything while sad, angry, frustrated or while experiencing ANY negative emotion rarely ends well for you or anyone else on the receiving end. Consider the story of the Happy Chef/Angry Chef.

The Happy Chef

You are seated in a beautiful restaurant where you can actually see your meal being prepared through a window and even close range video. As you gaze through the kitchen window, you see a chef singing and whistling as she is happily going about her business. You see the care she takes with slicing the ingredients while paying close attention to every detail. As she is about to conclude her preparations, she gets a sudden twinkle in her eye and reaches for one more special spice. She smiles with a deep contentedness because she knows she just created an absolute masterpiece and can already see your reaction of pure bliss as you take the first bite!

The Angry Chef

As you look through the window you can see this chef mouthing words that would be bleeped out in even the most liberal TV shows. She is stomping around, banging this and that and as you see the zoomed in version of her preparations, she is carelessly tossing stuff into her pot. As she is chopping the ingredients she—OUCH!—accidentally cuts her finger, which brings on a barrage of more colorful metaphors. With blood on the knife, she continues to slice the remaining items and can't cook the food and throw it on the plate fast enough!

Which chef would you like to BE? Which meal would you eat?

When you act out of feeling good, you benefit not only yourself by creating a great product or service that you enjoy, but you also pass that feel-good vibe on to anyone else who may be on the receiving end—another one of life's 2-for-1 specials!

Find the love in your action (Reprise...)

When doing things that you may not naturally love but feel are important to do like paying bills, cleaning the house, etc., accentuate the positive so you can feel better doing these things and keep your Allowing stream flowing. For example:

When paying bills, use The Power of APPRECIATION to acknowledge that you are investing in your wonderful AC that is keeping you and your family cool, are able to live in a place that keeps you comfy and dry, have a vehicle that Allows you the freedom to go wherever you want to go, plus all of the wonderful things that those credit cards Allowed you to purchase this month, etc.

When cleaning, have a cleaning party! Light some candles, put on some music you REALLY like (I can suggest some <lol>!), keep your favorite beverage close at hand, wear something that makes you feel playful, pause every so often to dance around the room and even invite some friends over if you like!

If you are about to do something and just can't seem to feel good about it, you almost always have the option of stepping away from it for a few seconds, minutes or even a few days and coming back to it later when you CAN feel good doing it. Many times when I have Allowed myself to step away from a task that was starting to feel like **HHW** (Hell and High Water) and then approached it with clear vision, I would either come back to it with a whole new attitude and get great results, or discover that investing my time in said project would have been a huge waste of time and energy that would have actually moved me toward something I did NOT want! Remember "The Journey IS the Destination."

How you feel on the way to your desired result determines the overall quality and feeling of that result once you arrive.

I have discovered time and time again that if ever the journey starts feeling funky, it is best to pause and refocus.*

There can be a positive side and even joy in virtually ANY action if you are willing to look for it, but it is of course up to you. Would you rather feel good and Allow or...?

*There is the exception, of course, of being in a place of constant, persistent negative thought, where all of the flares and signals to help bring you back to feeling good have been ignored and you are now over the falls in a barrel, or as Abraham would say are "jumping out of an airplane at 20,000 feet with no parachute." There are, however, SO many opportunities to feel good long before that fate has been sealed that it would be downright silly to let things escalate to that level!

The Bottom Line on The Power of AUTHENTICITY

Just as I mentioned in the introduction of this book when referring to Allowing, it takes courage to walk your own path and expand your experience and expression of authentic success. When you consider, however, that your rewards are Allowing joy, empowerment, freedom, fun, prosperity, love, well-being and living the stuff your happily-ever-afters (and NOWs) are made of, the question really is how could you NOT?

Thanks for keepin' it real!

———

"...Authenticity, my life is my own,
Authenticity, I'm already home,
Authenticity, just who I intended to be:
Authentically me..."

from "Authenticity"
© 2012 T.T.R.H.

The Power of AUTHENTICITY: Allowing Power Tools

Ready to fully engage The Power of AUTHENTICITY? Here are some T-riffic tools to help you get back in touch with YOU:

Remember, for best results, focus on the tools that feel best to you now
(= give you a lighter feeling or sense of relief).

TOOL#1
THE 7-YEAR OLD EXERCISE

"I have infinite time, infinite money and the infinitely free mind of a child! What can I do with my time and my life?"

DO THIS:

When you want to discover more about your true passions, desires and the things that are part of enjoying YOUR journey

1. Write this statement and question down on a piece of paper/etc.:

"I have infinite time, infinite money and the infinitely free mind of a child! What can I do with my time and my life?"

2. Set a timer for 7 minutes.

3. Start the timer and write as fast as possible.

NOTHING is off limits and logic and reason need to play elsewhere for a while!

4. Repeat this process for 7 days.

5. At the end of 7 days, circle the top 3-5 things that keep showing up. These are passions.

Take notice of the top ten as well because these are fun things that are still wonderful to include in your life!

Everything on the list, however, can be like puzzle pieces to help you get more in touch with YOU.

This is a stream of consciousness exercise that can help to bypass the filters of "shoulds" and limitations, enable you to gaze into a window of your true heart's desires and move into absolute freedom—if you LET it.

Even after my first test run of this exercise several years ago, I discovered things about my true desires that stimulated a whole new thought process (and career!) for me and started me down the path of all I do today. I still do this exercise from time to time to check in with myself as it always offers something expansive, wonderful and insightful!

NOTE: Be sure to do this when you are already feeling good, as your emotional starting point will have a great influence over what you permit to be expressed.

For a personal example of this tool in action visit:
www.AllowingYourSuccess.com/SecretPages

- ☛ Then use the code AYS-tjitd
- ☛ Then choose ALLOWING Power Tools
- ☛ Then The Power of AUTHENTICITY
- ☛ Then TOOL#1: THE 7-YEAR OLD EXERCISE

TOOL#2
THE HEART OF THE MATTER

Dig in to discover what truly matters and to get to the heart of your desire

———◆———

DO THIS:

When you want to get to the HEART of your desire and the feeling you are really reaching for

1. Get out a sheet of paper, write down the following sentence and fill in the blanks:

"I want __1___ because this can lead me to/give me ___2___."

2. Copy the next sentence and fill in the first blank with your answer from #2 above. Do this as many times as needed until you get the whole picture of what your desire represents, find the underlying feeling/feelings, and feel like you've truly reached the heart of your desire.

"I want __2___ because this can lead me to/give me ___3___."

"I want __3___ because this can lead me to/give me ___4___."

"I want __4___ because this can lead me to/give me ___5___."

etc...

3. Identify and write down the heart of your desire.

Being able to go straight to the heart of the matter and this core feeling will be a HUGE player in aligning with and Allowing your intentions!! (More about this in the next chapter, The Power of OWNERSHIP)

For a personal example of this tool in action visit:
www.AllowingYourSuccess.com/SecretPages

- ☛ Then use the code AYS-tjitd
- ☛ Then choose ALLOWING Power Tools
- ☛ Then The Power of AUTHENTICITY
- ☛ Then TOOL#2: THE HEART OF THE MATTER

TOOL#3
ACTION WITH AUTHENTICITY

The journey IS the destination, so choosing actions that are in alignment with enjoying the journey NOW also leads to quality, excellence AND Allowing Your Success!

———◆———

DO THIS:

When you want to get back to enjoying the journey and to act in ways that are more efficient and effective

1. Follow the flow of INSPIRED action.

When you feel a strong and clear urge to take action that feels awesome, do it now if at all possible!

2. FEEL before you act.

Before taking any kind of action, especially something that truly matters to you, check your gut first. Just like with inspired action, if you feel a strong and clear urge to take action that feels awesome, do it now, but if not:

Wait.

or

Choose something else that DOES feel good to do now.

or

Opt to find the love in it before taking action.

3. Find the love in it.

See Chapter 1, The Power of FOCUS, TOOL#4:
DO WHAT YOU LOVE OR FIND THE LOVE IN IT.

The Power of Words:
Authentic Oratory

"To thine own self be true" is a great slogan for inner and outer communication. It truly is SO much easier to just be honest and genuine overall than to jump through hoops to please others or sling the ol' B.S.!

Instead of Faux-Phraseology	Use Authentic Oratory
He/she thinks I should...	I really like___.
I really should ____.	What feels good or really matters to me right now?
No one would like the real me.	I really like the idea of being with people who appreciate me for me.
It feels good to do what makes others happy and seeing the looks of approval and understanding in their faces.	It feels really good to do what makes ME happy and to be a living example of someone living an authentic, happy life. I love inspiring others to recognize their own power and joy!

The Power of Music for AUTHENTICITY

Download music for The Power of AUTHENTICITY
by visiting this link: www.AllowingYourSuccess.com/SecretPages

- ☛ Then use the code AYS-tjitd
- ☛ Then choose ALLOWING Music
- ☛ Then The Power of AUTHENTICITY
- ☛ Then click on the song title of your choosing and ENJOY!

*Thank you in advance for honoring and respecting the value of our work and using this code just for you and your household.

Additional Resources for
The Power of AUTHENTICITY

Movies, Books & Beyond:

Under the Tuscan Sun (film)

Cool Runnings (film)

Chocolate (film)

Swing (film)

Taos (film)

Living Luminaries (film)

Opa! (film)

5 Wishes (short film)

August Rush (film)

The Shift: Ambition to Meaning (film)

The Celestine Prophecy (film)

5 Wishes by Gay Hendricks

Jonathan Livingston Seagull by Richard Bach

The Passion Test by Janet Bray Attwood and Chris Attwood

Dandelion by Sheelagh Mawe

SoundsTrue.com (multiple titles, authors and resources)

Shambhala.com (multiple titles, authors and resources)

HayHouse.com (multiple titles, authors and resources)

Additional Resources for
The Power of AUTHENTICITY (continued)

Transformation-Publishing.com (multiple titles, authors and resources)

Your gut and inner guidance—THE best Authenticity gauge, EVER!

**To access our current list of ever-expanding resources visit:
http://AllowingYourSuccess.com/allowing_resources.php**

<u>Your Journey So Far:</u>

FOCUS
on the PRESENCE
of the BEAUTY
of your true NATURE
with APPRECIATION
for your AUTHENTICITY.

7. The Power of OWNERSHIP: Allowing Keys

Want your stuff NOW? Start by BEING the Destination!

Ownership and Allowing

OK you fabulous **CEO**s! This is the part where you get to be Dorothy stepping into OZ in Technicolor®! You've heard the supermodel talk— "Work it! Use it! OWN it!" Well, if you are wanting to Allow your stuff and experiences pronto, OWNERSHIP (of your *joy* and *true self*) is the name of the game!

Owners are Visionaries

A great quote from George Bernard Shaw that has inspired me for many years is:

"Most men see things as they are and say 'why?' I see things that never were and say 'why not?'"

If you are to have, experience, and most of all BECOME more, you must first open yourself up to the idea of what could be. According to Abraham-Hicks, 99.99% of what we want is done and complete the moment we identify it, whether we directly articulate it with our words or not! Your job is to simply harmonize with it by feeling good now and, when feeling really good, use visualization and virtual reality tools as extra fun ways to practice the living and having of it so it feels normal and natural when it shows up.

Feeling good and expanding your belief is the ticket, folks, and visioning work (vision boards, acting as if, etc.) can be a great Allowing tool. When you get to the point where your visions absolutely feel real, so much so that it feels like they are already here and you are not longing for, needing or missing them, you now begin to really BELIEVE that they are, and in so doing, bada-bing bada-BOOM! Voila! Presto! HERE they ARE! There is, however, an important point worth making when it comes to visioning work; if it ever feels like effort is required or you are not feeling good at the time, this is not the time to play this game. Engaging in visualizations and focusing on your intentions, etc. when you are not already feeling groovy can actually bring unnecessary resistance into the picture and slow your Allowing process down. For best results, simply opt to do whatever feels best to you in the moment to get back to enjoying your now. Visit with your virtual reality only when you've got good mojo flowing.

Owners take and have Response-ABILITY

Another aspect to being an effective owner/**CEO** is knowing that your life experience truly is your own creation and perception. Though funky things arise at times, it is actually far more empowering to know that you invited those experiences on some level for one reason or another, rather than blaming some creepy guy with a pitchfork lurking about calling the shots. You remember that this is your show (and Source is always standing at the ready to guide you home) and then you can just as quickly turn things around by opting to exercise your Power of FOCUS to feel better and choose something different! Using this logic, this means that you are responsible for all the GOOD that has come into your life too!

The great thing about being the **CEO** of your life experience and working with The Power of OWNERSHIP means that even though you may not have the (empty and fleeting) satisfaction of blaming other people or circumstances for the things you don't like, you never again play the role of a victim in ANY way, shape or form—EVER! You really know and understand that no one and nothing outside of yourself can ever prevent you from feeling good or experiencing living a life you love. Giving up blaming others and whining is a small price to pay in favor of having true creative control of your life and Allowing your greatest dreams and visions to come into being!

Owners appreciate what they DO have & enjoy the journey

The best owners on the planet truly appreciate what they DO have and are owners of joy with or without their stuff. Just like our story of Bob and Un-Bob in Chapter 4, The Power of APPRECIATION, there is no amount of wanting to be somewhere better that can make up for simultaneously hating where you are. When you resent and reject your now, you keep yourself in a perpetual tug of war with nothing to show for it but a few fleeting moments of happy daydreaming and your feet still solidly planted right where you are. If you move into a new job or relationship, it just so happens to have all the SAME funky elements as the one you just left! Taking a cue from Bob and finding a way to be cool with and appreciate where you are now gets you back in the feel-good flow and sends the vibe that you are ready to be promoted to something new and more!

Great CEOs have great REPs

When it comes to being a **CEO** who is large and in charge, it's all about getting a handle on your **REP** (Repeating Emotional Pattern). Those who tend to short circuit at the first onset of funkiness and let what is happening around them or who's doing what when dictate how they feel tend to have more of a victim **REP**. For them, success in any area is always contingent on being born under the right star or being favored by the powers that be, which massively slows everything down when it comes to Allowing success!

A **CEO** with a great **REP**:

- knows who s/he truly is.

- remembers the power s/he truly has.

- recognizes that the journey IS the destination.

- is a true leader who follows her/his inner guidance and acts from a place of real power.

- knows that these are the only things s/he need (or can) control or own.

CEOs with great **REPs** experience contrast just like everyone else, but consciously use their Power of FOCUS to get back in the groove of feeling (first) better, then good as soon as possible. They appreciate the good that already exists now and visit with their expanded reality as often as it lights their fire. They are rockin' the house, livin' large and benefit anyone who is fortunate enough to cross their path!

How to get a better REP? Simply play with ANY Allowing Power Tool in this book, because that is the intention behind each and every one! Who loves ya, baby?

Owners don't micro-manage

Detail is great when it comes to planning a party, serving a great meal or providing great customer service, but getting attached to exact dates, specifics of who will be involved, or determining exactly how your desire will manifest, can actually push your closing date further and further away and greatly limit your level of joy and success. As long as a certain degree of detail still feels good, light and exciting when you contemplate your desire *(like KNOWING your fab new car is a certain make, model and color!)*, go with it. Overall, however, it is always best to leave the finite details—especially the how part—to your Source and the Divine team who CAN orchestrate infinite possibilities for fabulousness while always keeping the **BPI** and your personal BIG picture in the equation!

Be patient (or better, Present!) as Ownership changes hands

Often times, once we've identified a new desire, we can't seem to have, experience or be it soon enough. We want it and we want it NOW, by gosh! The thing to remember here is when we have invested a great deal of time, energy and passion in our "old business" and developed a long-standing pattern of resistant thought, it may take time for ownership to change hands.

A quick shift is certainly not impossible (nothing is!) and CAN happen with quick and full releasing of resistance, followed by laser-focusing on how good it feels to be in your expanded reality and self. In most cases, though, we often need to be a little more patient* with ourselves when releasing old aspects of our lives or beliefs that have been with us for a long, long time. The key is once we've identified our new vision, honor every step of the journey, celebrate even the smallest victories and continue to focus on the aspects and FEELINGS associated with our new and improved lives, we then become the owners of who we truly are and what we truly love.

Remember, as mentioned in Chapter 2, The Power of PRESENCE, that when we are fully present and are enjoying the journey there is no need for patience!

Owners are Present

Once you are clear about where you are headed and what you want, it's just as important to pay attention to your NOW for clues that your intentions are on the way! Besides, if all you ever do is constantly ask, how can you ever hear the answer? This is another great reason to live in the present. HERE AND NOW IS WHERE THE ANSWERS LIVE!

Here's a joke that I think illustrates this point beautifully:

In the midst of a great flood a man prayed to God for help. The water continued to rise, so the man made his way to the roof of his house. As he gazed upon the rising water, a person in a canoe nearing the man's home invited the man to get in. The man simply replied, "No thanks, God will provide." A few minutes later a couple came by in a motor boat also offering the man a ride, to which he replied, "No thanks, God will provide." Now that the water was closing in on him, the man looked up and sure enough, there was a helicopter hovering above him with a rope and helper ready to lift the man to safety. To this, he again replied, "No thanks, God will provide."

After a few minutes, the water level rose above his head and the man drowned. When he arrived in heaven he asked to have an audience with God. His wish was granted and when he met God he asked, "Lord, I thought you would provide?" To this God said, "I sent a canoe, a motor boat, and a helicopter!!"

Symbols, answers and inspired ideas are all around us! Here's an example:

When I think about my journey of getting closer and closer to Allowing the relationship I now have with my husband, I am amazed by the many attributes the men I dated a few years prior to meeting my now hubby had in common with him! As a matter of fact, the only other person I had seriously considered marrying had identical handwriting and many personality traits in common with John! Comparing pictures of the two of them, one might even think they were brothers!! My point here is I was actually getting closer and closer to my Prince Charming with each relationship, with each one being a preview of coming attractions! By the time John showed up, I was primed and ready—so much so that when he proposed to me my answer was, "Absolutely!"

Watch for signs, notice things that remind you of your intentions and listen for the call of inspiration! Your dreams and visions may be even closer than you ever imagined!

Owners let it go to let it grow

Debbie Cohen, a great Mastermind teacher and coach, uses a wonderful metaphor:

Once you plant a seed, give it water, love and time. There's no need to keep digging it up. As a matter of fact, doing so may actually impede its growth or even prevent it from coming to fruition!

Know the difference between owning and obsessing. As with anything else, let your feelings be your guide. If you feel energized, light, happy and alive, you're definitely on the right track! If something has to happen for you be OK, there are consequences of some kind or there is a feeling of heaviness attached to it, it's time to cease and desist. There's also a natural indicator light within us that seems to turn on when you just KNOW whatever you want IS. In any case, there can be great power in looking at a particular intention—especially one that is longstanding— and simply saying to yourself, "That's a done deal," while moving on to something new. Sometimes letting go is that final Allowing piece that gives your sweet little bud the boost it needs to blossom into a prize-winning rose at the perfect time when its beauty is most radiant!

The Bottom Line on The Power of OWNERSHIP

When you stop and really consider the **BPI**, all intentions are really about creating an expanded version of YOU. Michael Bernard Beckwith, speaker, author, featured Secret teacher and Founder of the Agape Spiritual Center, starts his "Life Visioning Process" by helping listeners first tune in to who and what they want to BECOME in order to be in a position to receive their intentions. If the things you seek are the trappings of one who is confident, talented, empowered, loving and prosperity-minded, start with seeing and feeling YOURSELF as the true über-**CEO** you are. This is always the key to Allowing and accepting your stuff.

Remember Bob in Chapter 4, The Power of APPRECIATION? He was in a place of appreciation and went above and beyond what his job description required because it felt good to him to act more like a business owner than just a mail room clerk. This is what made him ready for that promotion!

The secret formula to living, being, doing, or having a bigger, more magical self and life beyond what we now know is to:

- remember that your life experience IS truly in your hands, heart and mind.

- see beyond what exists today into the possibilities of tomorrow.

- love the gifts that are present here and now.

This may sound like a tall order, but when you begin to see that The Power of OWNERSHIP is simply a dance where feeling good always leads, the music only gets sweeter at every turn!

...and isn't life more fun when you are light on your feet?

So good to be remembering...

"When I see the eagle rising in the sky,
I remember I was meant to fly..."

from "Remembering"
© 2011-12 T.T.R.H.

The Power of OWNERSHIP:
Allowing Power Tools

Ready to take the full leap to OWNING your power, fabulousness and visions? Here are some tools you can use to experience the outstanding Power of OWNERSHIP:

Remember, for best results, focus on the tools that feel best to you now
(= give you a lighter feeling or sense of relief).

TOOL#1
START AT THE TOP & TAKE IT UP WITH
THE MANAGEMENT

*For an upgraded life, start with the **CEO** (AKA YOU!)*

DO THIS:

*When you need to show the **CEO** a little more love or when you are ready to embrace the next version of YOU!*

1. Do the "Thanks for YOU" exercise (TOOL#4 in Chapter 4, The Power of APPRECIATION), or revisit your results to get some good mojo for the **CEO!**

2. Build the new **CEO**:

Get out a sheet of paper/etc. and write down the answer to these questions in the present and possessive (AKA ownership) tense:

Attitude: How does the expanded version of ME (who I truly Am) see life and the world?

I feel/know_____.

Vibe: How does the expanded version of ME (who I truly Am) feel day-to-day?

I feel_____.

Coolness Factor: What character traits does the expanded version of ME (who I truly Am) possess and express?

I Am_____.

Relationships: How does the expanded version of ME (who I truly Am) relate to others?

I_____.

For a personal example of this tool in action visit:
www.AllowingYourSuccess.com/SecretPages

- ☞ Then use the code AYS-tjitd
- ☞ Then choose ALLOWING Power Tools
- ☞ Then The Power of OWNERSHIP
- ☞ Then TOOL#1: START AT THE TOP

TOOL#2
THE WHOLE PIE

Want to stay on track? Get clear on your big picture!

DO THIS:

When you are wanting to get familiar with and into the great-feeling place of living your expanded self, dreams and visions and enjoy your journey now!

1. Do a little prep-work to get to feeling good.

Notice beauty, listen to music you enjoy, write down appreciation, etc. so ideas can flow easily.*

2. Find a quiet space where you have privacy.

Allow 5-20 minutes, depending on your comfort level and the amount of detail you choose to experience.

3. Close your eyes and see, hear, taste, touch and smell what your ultra-cool life is like.

If it helps you focus more clearly, and you would like something to refer to later, put it in writing. Here are a few key areas and ideas:

Physical body/overall well-being:

- how your body feels and functions.
- how your body looks.
- what you feel and experience emotionally.
- what you feel and experience spiritually.

Home - where and how you live:

- where you live.
- how your home(s) feels.
- what your home(s) look like inside and out.
- what the surrounding area looks/feels like.
- what you have in your home(s).

Career/What you spend your time doing:

- what you enjoy doing.
- what kind/how much prosperity/money/opportunity is flowing to you.
- what your work environment(s) looks/feels like.
- what type of people you work/co-create prosperity with.

Stuff/experiences/adventures:

- what kind of car(s) do you drive?
- where do you shop?
- what kind of clothes, shoes, accessories, etc. do you own/ wear?
- where do you travel? How do you travel? (cruise, 1st class air, road trips, etc.)
- what kind of things do you do for fun?
- what other kind of "toys" do you have? (RV, boat, Wii, etc.)

Relationships:

- describe your romantic relationship(s).
- what kind of friends do you have?
- what kind of relationships do you have with your children/ family?

As you do this, feel free to get as detailed as feels good to you. You may notice that it may feel better to stay more general or simply connect with an overall feeling on certain subjects. If this is the case, no worries!! Anything that feels good, no matter how general it is, is still moving you in the direction of more feel-good stuff! This is YOUR life and you are allowed to experience anything you choose! Feel free to make any upgrades or additions as you see fit to keep your whole pie FRESH and FUN. The key here is for this to be a feel-good activity and as long as you are feeling good, you are on the right track*!

*If, for any reason, you feel resistance to doing this or are not in what you would consider to be a relaxed state of mind or better, simply wait until you are in a good space before attempting this exercise.

TOOL#3
SMALL SLICES

Bite sized pieces can make every step a victory!

———◆———

DO THIS:

Every time you are preparing to take action and would like to take ownership of good experience!

1. Revisit TOOL#1: CHOOSE YOUR DESTINATION in Chapter 1, The Power of FOCUS.

I have used this tool to secure fabulous parking spots, get super seats to a show, have fun with my family, have great sex, compose effective e-mails, have fun and smooth recording sessions, you name it! Focusing on small slices keeps positive momentum flowing, ensures productivity, creates consciousness check-points for staying in the Allowing driver's seat AND helps us to enjoy now by relaxing when we are in the midst of activity! Yep, investing in the small slices can truly play a huge role in making The Power of OWNERSHIP *SOOOOOOO* sweet!

TOOL#4
FOCUSED INTENTION – WHAT AND WHY

Add power by prioritizing and focusing on the why

———◆———

DO THIS:

When there is a specific intention that you want to align with and get the feel-good wheels turning!

WHAT:

1. Choose an intention that feels doable and real to you.

The more possible it feels, the more easily you Allow it!

2. Put it in writing using the present tense, focusing on what you want.

Use ("I am," "I have," etc.) or even past tense (as in "done deal"!) and focus on what you want (rather than what you don't want) using positive language.

3. Add an emotional tag to your intention. For example:

I am so excited about _____.

I love _____.

I am so thankful for _____.

4. Take a moment to really visualize/own your intention/experience to make it real and done in your mind.

Sample intention:

I am SO loving my new job! I love doing what I get to do, love the people I work and interact with, love the feeling and beauty of the space I work/create in and love consistently Allowing the kind of income that lets me to easily be able to honor all of my commitments and live the type of lifestyle I love!

5. Opt to close your Whole Pie session with your focused intention (or, if you prefer or are short on time, even opt to base a full sensory experience around your focused intention only).

Repeat this process as long as it feels good to you or is complete.

WHY:

1. Get out a sheet of paper and write, "Why do I want insert your intention here?"

2. List all the reasons why you want what you want, especially adding how you will feel when you have it.

3. Review this list daily, even adding to it if you are inspired to do so.

This helps to keep you on the ownership (AKA feel-good) side of the equation concerning your intention.

Side Bar: Mastermind partner/groups

Having a partner who reads your intention daily and knows you as you TRULY are, or choosing to participate in a Mastermind group where all involved are coming together with the intention of amplifying one another's visions and intentions, is another stellar way to add more juice to owning your stuff! Whether it is the feel-good aspect of knowing others are holding the high ground on your behalf, or simply giving your intention more focused air-time for your benefit, masterminding with a partner or group can certainly be a powerful experience!

See Additional Resources for Mastermind group suggestions/ideas.

The Power of Words:
Owner's M.O.

*Shift from "I want" to "I AM" or "I HAVE." When do you want it?
NOW, of course! The sooner we IDENTIFY with it as
already existing—owning it rather just wanting it--
the sooner life delivers it!*

Instead of Wishful Whining	Try Owner's M.O.
Perhaps someday I'll get lucky enough to...	I really love knowing that I have the power to Allow ___ into my life at the perfect time!
How come s/he gets to have ___! It's not fair!	Look at that! There's another sign that it IS possible! Seeing other people having/doing ___ is a great sign that I'm on the right track!
I try so hard and nothing seems to work...	Now that I know that having what I want is more about feeling good now and taking action that feels good rather than trying hard, I already feel better about my intentions showing up!
I feel like my life will never change...	Change is the very NATURE of life, so by relaxing and letting go, I open myself up to Allowing the kind of changes I want at the ideal time.

The Power of Music for OWNERSHIP

Download music for The Power of OWNERSHIP
by visiting this link: www.AllowingYourSuccess.com/SecretPages

- Then use the code AYS-tjitd
- Then choose ALLOWING Music
- Then The Power of OWNERSHIP
- Then click on the song title of your choosing and ENJOY!

*Thank you in advance for honoring and respecting the value of our work
and using this code just for you and your household.

Additional Resources for
The Power of OWNERSHIP

<u>Movies, Books & Beyond:</u>

August Rush (film)

Cool Runnings (film)

Field of Dreams (film)

The Perfect Game (film)

Kung Fu Panda (film)

The Matrix (film)

The Wizard of Oz (film-musical)

Any book, DVD or audio book by Abraham-Hicks

The Life-Visioning Process (audio) by Michael Bernard Beckwith

Illusions by Richard Bach

The Circle by Laura Day

The Best Year of Your Life by Debbie Ford

Living Juicy by Sark

SoundsTrue.com (multiple titles, authors and resources)

Shambhala.com (multiple titles, authors and resources)

HayHouse.com (multiple titles, authors and resources)

Transformation-Publishing.com (multiple titles, authors and resources)

MastermindU.com - a great site for Mastermind resources

Additional Resources for
The Power of OWNERSHIP (continued)

AllowingAdventures.com – Allowing, Mastermind and travel!

To access our current list of ever-expanding resources visit:
http://AllowingYourSuccess.com/allowing_resources.php

<u>Your Journey So Far:</u>

FOCUS
on the PRESENCE
of the BEAUTY
of your true NATURE
with APPRECIATION
for your AUTHENTICITY
as you take OWNERSHIP of your joy.

8. The Power of HARMONY: Allowing Keys

The sweetest song of Allowing Your Success first begins with Harmony!

Harmony feels good

If you have ever heard any piece of music, it is certainly no stretch to note *(pun intended!)* how much color and beauty harmony lends to the result. When notes are in resonance and complement one another, all is right with the world and you *physically* feel good when you hear this. On the other hand, when something is even a wee bit off, you feel the dissonance and discord physically as well. It's no wonder then, when *you* are in harmony with *yourself* and have discovered harmony within all aspects of your life and relationships that you feel like singing!

Resonance & Harmony with SELF

Have you ever tuned an instrument (or listened as someone else has) and noticed that the closer it gets to being in tune, the more the sound will wobble and often get under your skin until a perfect match to the desired note is achieved? Have you noticed that sometimes when you are really close to aligning with something you want there can also be a little layer or experience of funkiness? The good news is, this is simply a matter of having clearly chosen a new note (intention) while still in some way hanging on to the old note (intention). Just like tuning an instrument, all you need to do is make small adjustments to keep moving in the direction of what feels better and better, then voila! Sweet resonance is yours!

So how do you harmonize with your SELF? Who or what exactly ARE you harmonizing with? Doesn't it take more than one part to create harmony?

In the simplest sense, you are harmonizing with your Source and the expanded version of yourself and your life. As with music, when you are in a state of harmony, you find yourself in the middle of a symphony of the highest order. Your mind is clear. Everything flows better. It is easy to appreciate life and others and focus on the positive aspects around you. Things fall into place. In essence, you feel like a rock star!!

Get in tune before harmonizing with others

When you expand your sound-scape to include harmonizing with other life aspects and relationships, harmonies sound SO much better when each note (and instrument) is in tune. Sometimes, however, even the most well-meaning of us put the proverbial cart before the horse, seeking harmony with others first rather than finding it within ourselves.

All you need to do is listen to a piece of music with even one instrument or vocalist out of tune, and it becomes glaringly obvious how greatly it effects the wholeness of the piece. Even those who are not musically trained find themselves tilting their heads, much like a puppy, or in extreme cases, even experiencing physical pain! It's no wonder that pain, sickness and dis-ease are also related to being out of tune (or tuned out)!

Instead of co-creating a hit song or musical masterpiece, sometimes people can find themselves in the midst of one awful, *looooooooong* drawn-out song. When you don't know or understand how to get in tune, it certainly makes sense that you may feel your only recourse involves drowning it out via drinking heavily, taking drugs or excessive medication, gambling, over-working, over-eating, over-shopping, etc. Though this approach may temporarily mute the problem, because the focus is more about *making it stop*, rather than *getting in tune*, this approach actually keeps the unwanted song alive longer while turning the volume UP! By first choosing to get in tune (or tuned in) you then have the power to change the song to something you enjoy!

Seek and maintain harmony within *yourself* first and foremost by following what feels best to YOU at any given time, THEN speak, act or join the band! This is why every Allowing Power Tool in this book is dedicated to helping YOU get in tune!

Find your point of Harmony between intentions & beliefs

Even though we are all moving toward more and more of a life of Allowing, there could be a "hard work is necessary" or an "I must do this to get that" belief system in place that is still quite pronounced and active. Even though I have seen SO much overwhelming evidence in my own life of Allowing, I have noticed that there are some areas where the "I must do this to get that" paradigm (as Bob Proctor would say) is still active in my life. When I have totally disregarded this in an effort to just "Allow it, dammit!" (resistance, ya think?), my journey is fraught with dissonance! What helps me get back to being in harmony is this: I simply decide to make peace with the fact that I'm still in the process of upgrading my beliefs and do what feels best to me at the time.

To upgrade your beliefs while finding your point of harmony between intentions and current beliefs, check out TOOL#2 below.

Dissonance has its place too!

OK, so every tune you ever play or experience should be in perfect harmony, right? Interestingly enough, sometimes some of the most beautiful musical works (and lives) have periods of *dissonance*. What gives?

Dissonance in a song can definitely get our attention and is even widely known to create a feeling of tension for the listener, but when the dissonance resolves into harmony, often you appreciate and enjoy the harmony that much more! As with dissonance in music, when *you* are in a state of resistance (feeling negative emotion of some kind) but then discover a way to feel better and get back to feeling good again, it is a sweet and deeply rewarding experience!

Dissonance is not the enemy. It merely gives you the opportunity and gift of helping you to get clear about what you truly want. It lets you know when you are out of tune with yourself by providing a point of contrast so you can then use your fantastical Power of FOCUS to get back in tune and take your life's song to an even higher level of magnificence!

Life (and music) without any dissonance would Bb (a little musical humor meaning "be flat") and boring—hardly the awesome Allowing adventure we signed up for! The sooner you make peace with dissonance and see it for what it is: ebony to the ivory, Yin to the Yang, chocolate to vanilla, etc., the sooner you get (and mostly STAY) in the groove of Allowing success! It really IS <u>all</u> good!

The Bottom Line on The Power of HARMONY

The key to harmonizing with Allowing ANY area of success (including having great relationships with others) is to first get in tune with your

SELF. When you prioritize enjoying the journey and remember that dissonance is simply an invitation to get back in the groove, you not only Allow yourself to soar with the song of YOUR greatest bliss, but also get to:

- BE a living, breathing example of harmony in action.

- help others to remember and listen for the call of their songs.

- offer a melody that only ADDS to the beauty of the songs of others.

- broadcast a masterful symphony which has the power to uplift anyone and everyone with ears to hear!

Now THAT's what I call music!

———

"You are the harmony when my spirit sings..."

from "My Holiday"
© 2009-11 T.T.R.H.

The Power of HARMONY: Allowing Power Tools

Here are a few more tools to get in the groove with The Power of HARMONY:

Remember, for best results, focus on the tools that feel best to you now
(= give you a lighter feeling or sense of relief).

TOOL#1
WALK TO THE BEAT OF YOUR OWN DRUM

Follow the music that YOU hear for the greatest experience of harmony!

DO THIS:

When you really want to get in tune (tuned-in) and harmonize with your authentic self

1. Use The Power of AUTHENTICITY to find your ever-expanding song (Chapter 6).

2. Use The Power of PRESENCE to listen for your song (Chapter 2).

3. Use The Power of OWNERSHIP to align with and LIVE your song (Chapter 7).

All you need to do is turn the dial on the radio, visit YouTube or look at a well-stocked CD collection to see that when it comes to music, variety is the name of the game! We do NOT all hear the same music or harmonize with the same types of music, experiences or types of relationships. The best way to achieve the greatest harmony with yourself (and then others) is to follow the beat of your OWN drum!

TOOL#2
HARMONIOUS BELIEF UPGRADE

Only YOU know what creates harmony for YOU

DO THIS:

When you want to act in harmony with your desired intentions and current belief and/or consciously upgrade to new beliefs faster

1. Identify your current belief:

At this moment I feel I need to_____ in order to achieve/have/be _____.

2. Identify your desired new belief:

A new belief I would prefer to embrace is _____.

3. Set a clear intention that you continue to find more and more evidence of your new desired belief in action.

4. Act in accordance to what feels right at this moment, while knowing you have already planted the seed for upgrading and changing your belief.

This one little power tool has made an astonishing difference in my ability to Allow success! Try it and you may just amaze yourself as well!

> For a personal example of this tool in action visit:
> www.AllowingYourSuccess.com/SecretPages

> - ☞ Then use the code AYS-tjitd
> - ☞ Then choose ALLOWING Power Tools
> - ☞ Then The Power of HARMONY
> - ☞ Then TOOL#2: HARMONIOUS BELIEF UPGRADE

TOOL#3
LOOK FOR COMPLEMENTARY NOTES IN OTHERS

For harmonious relationships, focus on where you blend and what good things that relationship adds to your life's song

---

DO THIS:

When you are looking to improve any type of relationship or take a good relationship to an even more joy-filled place

1. Get out a sheet of paper/etc and write down:

    *   The name of the person you are focusing on.
    *   What you enjoy/like most about them.
    *   How does s/he complement me and/or what good does s/he add to my life?

NOTE: *For best results, do this only when you feel clear, light and in a good-feeling state of mind.*

The Power of Words:
Talking In Tune

*Want to dance to the music of a life of Allowing Your Success?
Talk in tune by letting your words harmonize with who you truly
are and the life you truly deserve!*

Instead of Disturbing Dissonance	Talk In Tune
Times are hard, so I just need to take what I can get.	Evidence of wealth and well-being is always around us and I choose to harmonize with THAT!
I've always had to work hard to get anything I want.	Right now I'm cool with doing what makes the most sense and feels best for me, but know I am moving more toward embracing a new belief and lifestyle of Allowing success. I am open to letting THAT become my new belief!
To harmonize with others I need to do what I feel is best for them and would make them happy.	When I get in harmony with myself first, everyone I interact with gets the best of me and I'm a lot more likely to tune in to what is best for all of us as a whole.
Sometimes life feels like just the same old song.	I love knowing that I have the power to change my tune at any time!

The Power of Music for HARMONY

Download music for The Power of HARMONY
by visiting this link: www.AllowingYourSuccess.com/SecretPages

- ☛ Then use the code AYS-tjitd
- ☛ Then choose ALLOWING Music
- ☛ Then The Power of HARMONY
- ☛ Then click on the song title of your choosing and ENJOY!

*Thank you in advance for honoring and respecting the value of our work and using this code just for you and your household.

Additional Resources for
The Power of HARMONY

<u>Movies, Books & Beyond:</u>

Broken Hill (film)

August Rush (film)

My Big Fat Greek Wedding (film)

Sabah (film)

Secrets of Six-Figure Women by Barbara Stanny

True Balance by Sonia Choquette

SoundsTrue.com (multiple titles, authors and resources)

Shambhala.com (multiple titles, authors and resources)

HayHouse.com (multiple titles, authors and resources)

Transformation-Publishing.com (multiple titles, authors and resources)

Virtually any song or piece of music by Enya

Rockapella, a killer a capella vocal group!

Any music that makes your heart soar!

To access our current list of ever-expanding resources visit:
http://AllowingYourSuccess.com/allowing_resources.php

<u>Your Journey So Far:</u>

FOCUS
on the PRESENCE
of the BEAUTY
of your true NATURE
with APPRECIATION
for your AUTHENTICITY
as you take OWNERSHIP of your joy
and live life in HARMONY.

9. The Power of EXPRESSION: Allowing Keys

How we Express is how we Allow Success!

What does Expression have to do with Allowing Your Success?

Though one may be inclined to think that we primarily express ourselves through our words, EXPRESSION is who we ARE, what we DO, and WHY we exist.

We are each a unique EXPRESSION of our Source and it is through our very state of being, including how we choose to focus and express in the world, that we Allow our Success.

Expression IS life and existence as we know it

A few years ago, I read a very esoteric and fascinating book called The *Ancient Secret of the Flower of Life* by Drunvalo Melchizedek *(yes, it is a mouthful <lol>!)* One chapter focused upon the Egyptian mystery schools and what is called Sacred Geometry. For some reason, though I was never a fan of math and geometry, I was drawn this subject in a very powerful way. After reading a particular chapter, I got out of bed to go downstairs and suddenly noticed that the room I was in, and everything in it, including my little cat, was nothing more than connected points of light! It was like I was seeing the true structure of all that exists and, as a fan of the positive aspects of the *Matrix* movies, like I was seeing THE Matrix!

From there, my view expanded to go further and further outward to above the earth and then to somewhere way out in the Universe. At that moment, my immediate feeling was that anything my tiny little self could perceive as a problem was utterly inconsequential. From this vantage point, the only feeling I had was absolute peace and being-ness, what I later described as being in a state of pure love.

When my perspective shifted back to my normal awareness and surroundings, I had an incredible insight: Though being in a state of utter being is a place of absolute peace and love, being able to EXPRESS and EXPERIENCE love ADDS a whole new dimension TO LOVE! This, in my opinion *(so take it or leave it)* is why we are here—to be able to EXPRESS and EXPERIENCE all that we are and to continue to expand our EXPRESSION and EXPERIENCE beyond where we have been before! With this idea in mind, when we are expressing in a way that is in sync with LOVE, there is no greater way to enjoy the journey and ALLOW Success!!

While this spontaneous glimpse of sorts was certainly a profound experience, I also discovered that no mystical experience is required to be able to Allow success and connect with the feeling of who we truly are. We can do this at *any* time for *any* reason and find inspiration in even the simplest things:

> *"To see a world in a grain of sand*
> *And a heaven in a wild flower*
> *Hold infinity in the palm of your hand*
> *And eternity in an hour..."*
>
> *~William Blake~*

Day to Day Expression Matters: Expression is Powerful

In case you haven't noticed, we humans *LOOOOOVE* to express. We express our opinions, our thoughts, our dreams, our laughter, our ideas, our criticism, our creativity, our sorrow, our joy and everything in-between. We are simply one big ball of expression! This definitely serves us well when we are expressing and sharing ideas that feel good.

Unfortunately, however, we can hang out on the side of auto-pilot parroting and simply repeat what we have heard on the news or rehash a problem that we or someone else is experiencing. We then discuss why it is SO very bad in detail and get others' opinions about it until it just gets bigger, hairier and scarier! It is understandable in one way, since we are naturally curious creatures who like to collect data. In contrast, if we were to instantaneously replace the expression and exploration of the icky-feeling stuff with GOOD-feeling stuff, there would literally be a shower of all things auspicious falling en masse as far as the eye could see and shouts of sheer bliss as far as the ear could hear!

FEEL before you speak

We've all heard the phrase "Think before you speak." but sometimes our thoughts can come so quickly it's hard to really stay on top of them. Plus, attempting to monitor every little thought would greatly inhibit our ability to enjoy the journey. A better way to know if you are moving toward something cool and are about to express something that is brilliant, in alignment with who you truly are, and beneficial for the party on the receiving end, is to simply take a moment and let your feelings be your guide.

When you feel good (or better than you did before), your natural inclination is to express something that is in harmony with good mojo for the benefit of all. When you don't feel so hot, you are far more likely to express something that moves you in a different direction than you would have preferred. Like catching and releasing an unpleasant thought that just happened before it gathers any real momentum, so much negativity can be missed entirely if you feel before you speak or only initiate and participate in conversations (with others or internally) that feel GOOD!

Deposit or Withdrawal?

Think of it this way: Expressing what feels good such as creating, sharing and appreciating beauty or praising what you DO like = deposit, whereas commiserating, complaining, or criticizing = withdrawal. Like the idea of a balance (life or bank account) with positive flow? Choosing to take a moment to feel before you speak and express with the intention of *increasing* good is a great way to Allow success on many fronts while positively influencing your fellow travelers. Bonus!

EI: Express to Increase & Allow Success!

Expression (a version of our Power of FOCUS) is kind of like "The Force" in Star Wars. It can be used as a phenomenal Allowing tool or take you on a trip to "The Dark Side." If you remember Anakin, who later becomes Darth Vader, it's clear that The Dark Side leads anywhere BUT to joy, freedom and bliss.

Knowing that what you focus on is what you choose (and become) and expressing <u>anything</u> in <u>any way</u> is one of the ways you focus, imagine how awesome your life would be if you only expressed fabulousness!

What if all people used their Power of EXPRESSION for expanding beauty and inspiration in the world?

Though variety is the spice of life and there will always be many different forms and types of expression, what if you only amplified the best in others? What if you created and focused on the beauty that IS a part of our world, or even consistently offered a simple smile? Yes, it's true that we only have control over our own experience, but putting positivity out into the word gives anyone who is open to it a wonderful opportunity to feel better.

Considering that one person crosses paths with several, even hundreds of other human beings on a daily basis, who also cross paths with several, even hundreds, and so on, it is amazing to know that it only takes one of us to positively and directly influence thousands, even millions of lives in the course of a single day! Now that's what I call Allowing success and sharing the love, baby!!

*See Part 2: **EI:** Express to Increase in the Power Tools below for ways of using your Power of EXPRESSION to Allow your success!*

Expression is powerful but...

Our dominant vibe and habit of thought always rules regardless of what may be spoken and expressed. ALL of us as human beings and powerful **CEO**s have the ability to focus and take only the good stuff from our interactions with others. We each have our own unique lens based on our personal perception of the world and whatever emotional state we may be in at any given time (Don Miguel Ruiz, author of The Four Agreements calls this a "mitote" or personal dream). No amount of harsh words we utter can truly rock the boat of someone who is solid in her/his joy and power, and even the most well-meaning complement or innocuous "hello" can be misinterpreted by someone who is in a state of self-loathing and despair.

The thing to know about emotional states (AKA vibes) is this: We each need to be close enough to a certain state of feeling/being to be able to get or receive a message. The further away we are, the more it is as if we are speaking completely different languages. For example, have you noticed that:

When you feel really confused and frustrated and have lost something, you often find it once you are feeling better, and it is typically in an obvious place where you may have even looked right at it but did not see it?

While re-listening to an audio-book, you often hear new things that you didn't catch last time, sometimes even to the point of feeling like "that wasn't there before!"?

If you're in a sad or angry state of mind, the LAST thing you want is a cheerleader bouncing up and down in front of you shouting pretty, perky, positive words at you?

During times you are truly in harmony with yourself and feel amazing, things that used to bug you before aren't even a blip on your radar, and you now find them cute and even truly appreciate them?

Political correctness rarely leads to any level of true connection or joy for anyone on either side of the table?

Give yourself the gift of freedom by making peace with the fact that you cannot control the lens of another person's experience, period. Understand that expressing to increase is all about using your Power of EXPRESSION to stay in harmony with YOUR best self and experience so when you do interact with others, you continue to feel good AND put the good vibrations out there for anyone who IS in a place to receive them. It feels good to feel good and, I don't know about you, but the feeling of expressing something that could also potentially uplift a fellow traveler adds icing to the cake, sprinkles and a cherry on top of the feel-good extravaganza, hence an all-out Allowing par-tay!! SWEET baby!

ER: Express to Release

Expressing to increase IS certainly the name of the game when it comes to Allowing success, but what is there to do when a sudden and big piece of contrast shows up on our doorstep or we've Allowed ourselves to tangle with the dark side for more than a few minutes? At times when I have taken off on the proverbial side road and managed to generate oodles of negative emotion, I've found that sometimes the best way out is actually *through*. Rather than try to *make* myself feel good, I've discovered that going ahead and *letting* myself feel, express and release those strong uncomfortable emotions fully and completely can actually be the fastest route back to feeling good.

177

Suppression, which is a form of resistance, is NEVER a healthy way to get back to Allowing. In fact, suppression actually causes those unwanted things to gain even greater power, often resulting in an explosion/implosion that culminates in an involuntary breakdown of well-being on many fronts. Many teachers and health practitioners also agree that suppressed emotion (much like dissonance) is at the heart of virtually every form of dis-ease. My point here is simply this: Always do your best to turn in the direction of what feels better first, but during times where nothing seems to work, sometimes it's best to go for some good **ER**.

Go to "The River" for Express Check Out!

Just like going to the ACTUAL Emergency Room is seen as a last resort and we prefer not go on a frequent basis or book an extended-stay experience there, the trick is to get in and get OUT! The Law of Attraction is still doing its thing 24/7 whether we are feeling warm-and-fuzzy or not, so keep the scales tilted on the positive side of the equation by keeping your Express and Release visits short and maintaining an overall good **REP**. The key to a QUICK visit? Go to The River by immersing yourself in whatever you're feeling and give it ALL you've got!

I can speak only for myself, but whenever I have given myself license to say and feel ANYTHING without judgment or limitation, even letting myself hate something, I have literally been able to go from a place of deep sorrow or anger to a place of peace and even appreciation within HOURS and even MINUTES (when such emotional journeys would take days or even weeks in the past!).

The ONLY reasons anything ever becomes a lingering miserable melodrama is because we either keep the negative aspects of our experience vibrantly active through our thoughts, words/conversations and actions, or we just don't let ourselves fully release what we truly feel. Like many, I too have experienced contrast of an extremely high order in my life, but I have discovered that ALL negative emotions can and do pass. Even during times when I thought I could NEVER feel good again, I always found my way back to joy, and so can you, my dear friend!

*When you feel the need for some **ER** time, use the tools in Part One – ER: Express to Release below.*

Expression and The Power of Music

Although I have already dedicated an entire section to The Power of MUSIC in Section III, Allowing Foundation, this über-tool can be an outstanding way to work with either side of the expression coin (**ER** or **EI**). On the **ER** side, a little catharsis certainly is good for the soul from time to time and every one of us has felt the relief a sad or angry song can provide.

When it comes to **EI,** singing along with, composing, dancing to or listening to feel-good, positive music may very well be one of the coolest and most effortless means for Allowing that I share in this book! Because music with positive lyrics can speak to both the intellect and the heart, this universal medium can be MASSIVE in your quest to express to INCREASE!! If you have downloaded and listened to the songs accompanying the chapters of this book so far, you have already had a glimpse of the power of feel-good music in action! Being that feeling good is such a BIG part of Allowing, how cool is it that it really can be THAT easy!

The Bottom Line on The Power of EXPRESSION

Remember that we are each both EXPRESSIONs of our Source and **CEOs** who have the ability to express and experience the very best of ourselves and our lives if we choose to do so. Choosing to use our power of EXPRESSION to increase the good in our lives and be a true positive influence for others is what separates the women from the girls and the men from the boys...

...but when you discover what it feels like to inhabit a life that greets you with warm welcomes and smiles seemingly everywhere you go, are Allowing Your Success on a consistent basis and feeling like The Force is always with you, it's only natural to want to shout it out, baby!

Sing it with me now:

"I'm movin' groovin' shakin' baby, living my dreams—oh yes I am!"

from Groovin' on Life!
© 2009-12 T.T.R.H.

The Power of EXPRESSION:
Allowing Power Tools

Joy, freedom and bliss, like them you do? (as Yoda would say) Here are some Power Tools for truly "Groovin' on Life!" and using The Power of EXPRESSION for Allowing The Force to be your friend:

Remember, for best results, focus on the tools that feel best to you now
(= give you a lighter feeling or sense of 'relief').

PART 1: ER (Express to RELEASE)

TOOL#1
GO TO THE RIVER FOR EXPRESS CHECK OUT!

*Go to The River and keep **ER** visits short for a quick return to well-being!*

—————◆—————

DO THIS:

When you've tried to do all you can to feel better, but have not felt any shift yet

1. Keep **ER** time private.

Find a place where you can be alone so you are free to say and do (or even write down if that is more appropriate at the time) whatever you choose.

OR

Consult your "Specialists"—people you love and trust who can Allow YOU 100%.*

Remember to honor your Specialists. Ask permission by letting them know that you need some **ER time. By doing this, you give them a moment to set their intentions to hold the high ground for you and be a catalyst for your quick **ER** visit or to opt out if they are in a place where they are in middle or even low ground themselves.*

2. Intend to release.

Set an intention before you go to The River to quickly release negative emotions with the intention of feeling better. I will sometimes even say out loud, "I'm ready to let go of these heavy emotions and feel better!"

3. Feel with ALL you've got until you experience some kind of release and relief.

For me, once I let myself cry, I reach a turning point and start to feel much lighter.**

4. Let yourself be comfortably numb after your release.

Just breathe and/or use one of the Power Tools from Chapter 2, The Power of PRESENCE to simply be.

5. When you feel ready (and you'll know if it feels good to do this), start thinking about what you want and why you want it.

Speak it out loud, or even better, write it down. The sooner you can comfortably accentuate the positive by keeping your focus on what you want and why you want it, the faster you get back on track to being your fabulous, joyful self and Allowing Your Success!

You will find that in no time, you will not only be back to feeling good but also have the bonus of knowing that YOU were the one who brought yourself back to joy, a sure way to really KNOW your true power as a **CEO!**

***It is, of course, best to just let this process unfold naturally without time constraints, but if you feel like you can only carve out a limited time for **ER** and have been going to The River a lot (especially in the case of a death or intense piece of contrast), set a time limit and stick to it. If, however, you REALLY let yourself have one good go, you may find that repeated visits to The River may not even be necessary. Above all, remember it's your party and you can cry as much and as often as you want to.*

TOOL#2
TANTRUM OR DRUM TO RELEASE!

Shake things up to let things go and lighten up!

DO THIS:

If you are more in a place of frustration/annoyance and want to loosen and lighten up

1. Just like TOOL#1: GO TO THE RIVER... above, start by setting an intention to feel better.

2. Find a place where you can be alone or invite one of your Specialists to participate with you.

3. When you are ready, yell, scream and jump up and down like a little kid who wants her/his ice cream NOW!!

OR opt for Drumming:

When you are ready, beat on a drum to your heart's content and yell, scream or make whatever crazy, silly sounds you choose to accompany your drumming session!!

4. Once you start laughing and feel lighter, try Steps 4 and 5 in TOOL#1 above.

PART TWO: EI (Express to INCREASE):

TOOL#1
TELL A NEW STORY OF Allowing Your Success

You ARE the CEO, after all!

DO THIS:

To add even more mojo to enjoying the journey and aligning with your Whole Pie (see Chapter 7, The Power of OWNERSHIP)

1. Put your Whole Pie in writing.

Write a personal life script or a *Rolling Stone Time, Life, Success,* etc. magazine article about your fabulous self and life (and if you chose to plug me or this book, I would be honored <lol!>). Make a note of:

- how much you are enjoying your amazing life, stuff and experiences.

- how success, in all areas, seems to be attracted to you like a magnet.

- how wonderful YOU are as a human being.

- how much of an inspiration you are to others!

TOOL#2
BECOME AN ALLOWING EVIDENCE COLLECTOR OR REVISIT YOUR ALLOWING EVIDENCE!

Focus on evidence of Allowing and Allow more in your own experience!

DO THIS:

When you want to fan the fires of your belief that success-through-Allowing IS possible and keep the feel-good flow happening!

1. Go on a mission to find and collect stories of Allowing success.

You can start your journey by visiting:
www. http://AllowingYourSuccess.com/true_stories.php

Here you will find real stories from real people who have Allowed success on a variety of different subjects including joy-filled careers, artistic brilliance, money, great relationships, health and well-being, stuff and adventures, and beyond!

2. Put the good stuff in writing:

*   share appreciation daily (see Chapter 5).

*   keep and review a daily Beauty List (see Chapter 3).

*   construct your own Allowing Evidence by revisiting and writing down one of YOUR stories of Allowing success.

As you write about your Allowing Evidence experience, be sure only to touch on the contrast that inspired it and really emphasize the joy in the journey and the synchronicities, signs and surprises you experienced along the way!* Telling your own Allowing story is a powerful reminder that you have and CAN Allow success into your life, plus focusing on a story of Allowing and revisiting the joy you felt gets you into a feel-good Allowing flow NOW!

If you have an Allowing story from your past or a new Allowing story that you have experienced as a result of reading this book that you would like to share, you may get your story published on our website and Beyond!

For information and to submit your story, e-mail:
Story@AllowingYourSuccess.com

TOOL#3:
DRUM TO INCREASE!!

Beat the drum (literally) of what you want!

———————◆———————

DO THIS:

When you want to beat the drum of enjoying your journey, engage in the present moment, amplify good feelings and celebrate life!

1. Drum with intention:

Start with an intention to drum for prosperity, well-being, gratitude, love, etc., then take a cue from indigenous people everywhere who have used drumming for prayer and celebration for millennia to connect with the heartbeat of Mother Earth and eternal celebration of life! You can even add a fun little chant or affirmation like, "I feel good, I knew I could!" or "prosperity is here with me!" or participate in a feel-good drum circle to enjoy the vibe of creating positive rhythms together!

Contrary to using drumming as a form of release, it can also be an awesome, fun, feel-good tool to send out a sonic BOOM in the name of intention, celebration and Allowing! Add to this that drumming is also a phenomenal tool for engaging in the present moment and letting the Allowing party to begin!

TOOL#4
EXPRESS YOUR WHAT AND WHY

When you'd like to feed good mojo and stay in the flow of Allowing fabulousness!

———◆———

DO THIS:

When you want to beat the drum of enjoying your journey, engage in the present moment, amplify good feelings and celebrate life!

1. Revisit TOOL#4: FOCUSED INTENTION—WHAT AND WHY in Chapter 7, The Power of OWNERSHIP for a great way to use expression to INCREASE the good!

TOOL#5
CREATE AN EXPRESSION OF BEAUTY

Create, express and share something beautiful for the benefit of all!

———◆———

DO THIS:

When you'd like to express and create something beautiful, enjoy the journey and be an inspiration for others

1. Revisit TOOL#4: CREATE SOMETHING BEAUTIFUL in Chapter 3, The Power of BEAUTY.

TOOL#6
FEEL BEFORE YOU SPEAK

How you feel lets you know whether you are about to make a deposit or withdrawal

---◆---

DO THIS:

Any time you are preparing to communicate and are feeling anything other than solidly clear and fabulous

1. Simply take a moment to check in with yourself (see how your gut and body feel) before expressing, especially when feeling less than your awesomely awesome self.

Choose to make a DEPOSIT (a statement of sincere appreciation, praise, etc.) if at all possible, or enjoy the silence rather than make or participate in a WITHDRAWAL (a statement of criticism or that emphasizes what you don't like).

The Power of Words:
Exceptional Expression

Expression is POWERFUL!
BE an expression of and catalyst for all-things-fabulous!

Instead of Disturbing Dissonance	Talk In Tune
How can I relate to others if I don't whine with them?	I really love being the one people come to when they have good news to share or genuinely want to feel better. It's nice being a catalyst for joy.
Positive talk is just a way of lying to yourself.	Choosing to focus on things I want, like and DO feel good about is a great way to draw more good stuff to me!
If there's no drama or struggle people won't be interested in my story or ideas.	The thought that life can actually be fun and that success can be Allowed can be a huge ray of hope and an inspiration to millions who want to enjoy their lives.
We must raise awareness about this horrible epidemic so it can be fought and stopped!	I know there is an answer here and I'm going to do all I can to stay focused on what want so I can then discover an awesome solution!

The Power of Music for EXPRESSION

Download music for The Power of EXPRESSION
by visiting this link: www.AllowingYourSuccess.com/SecretPages

- ☛ Then use the code AYS-tjitd
- ☛ Then choose ALLOWING Music
- ☛ Then The Power of EXPRESSION
- ☛ Then click on the song title of your choosing and ENJOY!

*Thank you in advance for honoring and respecting the value of our work
and using this code just for you and your household.

Additional Resources for
The Power of EXPRESSION

Movies, Books & Beyond:

ALL movies and books mentioned in this book plus:

Conversations with God (film) - EI and ER

The Moses Code (film-documentary) – EI

One (film-documentary) – EI

Black Whole (film-documentary, fascinating and inspiring!) – EI

Listen to Your Heart (film) – EI and ER

The Artist's Way by Julia Cameron – EI and ER

Conversations with God series of books
by Neale Donald Walsch – EI

Chicken Soup for the Soul series
by Jack Canfield and Mark Victor Hansen – EI and ER

All books, audio programs or DVDs by Abraham-Hicks - EI

All books by Og Mandino – EI and ER

All books by John Harricharan – EI and ER

All books by Deepak Chopra – EI (some ER)

All books by Wayne Dyer – EI (some ER)

SoundsTrue.com (multiple titles, authors and resources) – EI and ER

Shambhala.com (multiple titles, authors and resources) – EI and ER

HayHouse.com (multiple titles, authors and resources) – EI and ER

Additional Resources for
The Power of EXPRESSION (continued)

Transformation-Publishing.com
(multiple titles, authors and resources) – EI and ER

Mike Dooley's "Notes From The Universe"
http://www.tut.com/resources/notes/
(inspiring daily e-mails) – EI

DailyWord.com (daily inspiration from Unity) – EI

VenusJones.com (stirring spoken word artist and poet) – EI and ER

MoxyWomen.com
(site dedicated to empowering and inspiring women) – EI and ER

The Out Your ego! Series – divination cards, book, board game
www.StaciB.com – EI and ER

SpiritualCinemaCircle.com (monthly film club that brings inspirational
films with heart and soul to your door!) – EI and ER

AllowingYourSuccess.com (words, music, adventures and beyond
dedicated to Allowing) – EI

Music – for all reasons and seasons! EI and ER

To access our current list of ever-expanding resources visit:
http://AllowingYourSuccess.com/allowing_resources.php

<u>Your Journey So Far:</u>

FOCUS
on the PRESENCE
of the BEAUTY
of your true NATURE
with APPRECIATION
for your AUTHENTICITY
as you take OWNERSHIP of your joy
and live life in HARMONY
as a magnificent EXPRESSION of good.

10. The Power of HUMOR: Allowing Keys

Lighten up and let the good times roll!

Laugh your way to Allowing Your Success!

Have you ever noticed how powerful a good laugh can be, even in the midst of the most tense situations? Tense muscles and intense laughter simply cannot co-exist because laughter literally shakes you loose—and where there is no tension (AKA resistance), there is Allowing, baby!

Find the Humor

The only tragedy of life is it was meant to be a comedy! Life is hilarious! Simply watch kids, teenagers, pets, animals in general, or observe the wacky things your loved ones do. Sit in a cafe and people-watch or listen to the crazy stuff on TV, radio and in print ("Aliens ate my dog!"). I know when I stop to think about some of the silly things I've done, I find endless material for giggles in my very own back yard! It's really no stretch to hone in on the humor of life!

One trick I have used when finding myself in the presence of others who complain incessantly (fortunately, quite a rare occurrence these days!) is to pretend I am a stand-up comedian who is looking for great material for my next show. When I'm really on my game, I'll even take notes and (when I think I can get away with it), I'll even say, "That's good! I'll have to use that sometime!" This typically results in quizzical looks from my complaining friend and many times even prompts a change of subject! I can even recall countless times during very intense events— funerals, hospital visits, being liberated from a job, etc.—when an unexpected bit of humor felt like it literally helped me breathe again.

A great scene from the movie *Cheaper by the Dozen* starring Steve Martin involves two of his children doing something quite awful to their older sister's boyfriend. During his required dad reprimand, he tells the children that what they did was horribly wrong, "...funny, but wrong!" It's a line my husband and I steal any time we catch ourselves finding humor in dark situations, and it never fails to produce a much-needed chuckle!

Use a little "Ridiculous" magic

There's a great scene in *Harry Potter and the Prisoner of Azkaban* where the "Defense Against the Dark Arts" teacher instructs his students to picture something silly in place of something frightening. Every time I think about it, I can't help but smile at the brilliance of this simple and very *real* magic. While it certainly can take some focus to transform a fear or past memory into something ridiculous, infusing humor to lighten up and break the spell of a negative trigger is certainly worth the effort. Why is this so effective? When you can laugh at something, it no longer has power over you!

More about this in TOOL#3 below.

Past "Out-Takes" instead of mistakes

A great way to get back on the Allowing track when you stumble across an unpleasant memory is simply to stop and acknowledge it as one of my "out-takes" rather than a mistake.

This puts things in a whole new light and also helps to drive the point home that you and the other party/parties were simply playing out roles. This is also a great way to see the other party/parties as the complete and healthy souls they truly are behind the curtain of life. Lighten up the energy, feel better. It really is that simple!

See TOOL#3, step 2 below

Increase your Humor RDA

There's a reason for the saying "laughter is good medicine!'"

There are several accounts of individuals with a laundry list of health concerns—even cancer patients—who simply wrote themselves humor and laughter prescriptions and managed to heal themselves. How is that possible, you ask? By completely withdrawing their attention from the dis-ease (as Bob Proctor would say), and focusing on something that is all about ease and letting go (AKA laughter), they ceased resisting their wellness, and therefore started Allowing their wellness. It is truly amazing how lightening up can actually help us to reconnect with our power!

BTW...

Just for kicks I did a Google search on laughter as medicine (without quotes) and turned up 3,850,000 results! I don't know about you, but that's more evidence than I could ever need to prove this point.

Suggestions for increasing your humor RDA can be found in TOOL#4 below.

The Bottom Line on The Power of HUMOR & the punch line

The less seriously you take the game of life, the better you feel, the more fun you get to have, and the more you Allow Your Success! Sometimes the simplest truths are the most profound.

Funny isn't it?

———

"The only tragedy of life you see is it was always meant to be a comedy..."

from "I Came to Play"
© 2012 T.T.R.H.

The Power of HUMOR: Allowing Power Tools

Here are some Power Tools you can use to lighten up and harness the healing power of HUMOR:

Remember, for best results, focus on the tools that feel best to you now
(= give you a lighter feeling or sense of relief).

TOOL#1
WAKE UP LAUGHING

A little levity goes a long way!

DO THIS:

When you need to lighten up and loosen up

1.   Intend to focus on humor, recall something funny or watch or
     listen to something that makes you giggle.

On days when waking up with beauty or presence may feel like a bit
of a stretch to you emotionally, intending to focus on anything funny
or humorous can be just what the doctor ordered! Start to reach for
thoughts of anything you find funny or even put on a funny video or
CD to start your day on a lighter foot.

TOOL#2
FIND THE HUMOR

The only tragedy of life is forgetting it is meant to be a comedy!

————————

DO THIS:

When you're ready to start feeling better about life overall

1. Make it your mission to find something funny about whatever you are observing, as if you are a professional comedian looking for material.

Write down, photograph or film (when appropriate) anything that truly tickles your funny bone. Revisit your material any time you need a reminder of how funny life truly is!

NOTE: *Keep your material light. Sometimes comedy can be a double-edged sword that actually amplifies UNwanted things, so be sure to stay tuned-in to what truly feels better and lighter to you.*

TOOL#3
USE A LITTLE "RIDICULOUS" MAGIC

Infuse humor to defuse fears and bad re-runs

DO THIS:

When you'd like to get back to feeling good and transform the feeling around an unpleasant memory

1. Give an old memory or a fear a new voice or identity.

When recalling a bad re-run, try giving the voices in your head high-pitched helium-balloon-induced speech, or start skipping around the room in circles singing tra-la-la. Give a fear a silly new identity, wacky wardrobe or play it out in the context of a ridiculous old silent-movie-type melodrama. Visualize really bad actors playing out a low-budget B-movie type script using exaggerated facial expressions with really goofy music playing throughout!

The more twisted (uh, creative) your sense of humor, the easier it is to completely shift the energy around a past memory or fear!

2. Create Past Out-Takes instead of Mistakes.

When recalling an incident, see the participants in the scene—including yourself—as actors reciting lines, then going blank and saying stuff like, "Damn, I think I was supposed to yell, but I forgot my line!" then having a laugh and talking about meeting for lunch in your trailer later.

TOOL#4
INCREASE YOUR HUMOR RDA

There's a reason for the saying "Laughter is good medicine!"

—————◆—————

DO THIS:

When you want to lighten up or just enjoy the journey more

1. Start, end or fill your day with laughter!

    - watch a funny movie.
    - observe animals, children or babies playing or simply doing what they do.
    - read a funny article.
    - recall funny stories or jokes.
    - look at funny photos.
    - get on YouTube and type in "comedy," "funny videos" or keyword your fave comedian.
    - review any of your material when doing the FIND THE HUMOR... exercise above.

The Power of Words:
Light-Hearted Lingo

*Allow the good stuff AND be the life of the party
when you keep it light!*

Instead of Serious Sour-Puss	Use Light-Hearted Lingo
There's nothing funny about today's world.	All I have to do is look just about anywhere to see life is hilarious!
Life is serious business.	My life and business work better when I DON'T take them too seriously.
Pain is no laughing matter.	...It is when you laugh until it hurts!
We've decided to get serious about this relationship. (It's no wonder so many relationships go south!)	We've decided to spend more time together and have more fun!

The Power of Music for HUMOR

Download music for The Power of HUMOR
by visiting this link: www.AllowingYourSuccess.com/SecretPages

- ☛ Then use the code AYS-tjitd
- ☛ Then choose ALLOWING Music
- ☛ Then The Power of HUMOR
- ☛ Then click on the song title of your choosing and ENJOY!

*Thank you in advance for honoring and respecting the value of our work
and using this code just for you and your household.

Additional Resources for
The Power of HUMOR

<u>Movies, Books & Beyond:</u>

Shrek (film, entire film series)

The Producers (film)

Cheaper by the Dozen (films)

The American Pie Series (film)

The Birdcage (film)

The Hangover (film)

Bill & Ted's Excellent Adventure (film)

Trading Places (film)

Cool Runnings (film)

The Wedding Singer (film)

Wayne's World (film)

The *Austin Powers* series of films

Van Wilder (film)

Abbot & Costello series of films

SoundsTrue.com (multiple titles, authors and resources)

Shambhala.com (multiple titles, authors and resources)

HayHouse.com (multiple titles, authors and resources)

Transformation-Publishing.com (multiple titles, authors and resources)

Additional Resources for
The Power of HUMOR
(continued)

Seriously... I'm Kidding audio book by Ellen DeGeneres

Jeff Dunham - comedian

The Blue Collar Comedy Tour

Louis Black - comedian

Gabrielle Inglesias - comedian

Bill Cosby - comedian

Robin Williams - comedian

Weird-Al – song parodies (my personal favorite parodies are "Amish Paradise," "All About the Pentium," "White and Nerdy")

Whose Line is it Anyway? TV show hosted by Drew Carey— hilarious!!

Comedy Central

BBC Comedy

To access our current list of ever-expanding resources visit:
http://AllowingYourSuccess.com/allowing_resources.php

Your Journey So Far:

FOCUS
on the PRESENCE
of the BEAUTY
of your true NATURE
with APPRECIATION
for your AUTHENTICITY
as you take OWNERSHIP of your joy
and live life in HARMONY
as a magnificent EXPRESSION
of good HUMOR.

11. The Power of TRUST: Allowing Keys

Trust is a MUST for Allowing Your Success!

A Powerful five-letter word...

TRUST: This potent five-letter word evokes many different meanings and feelings. With so many flaky people and so much uncertainty in the world at large, who or what is one to trust? Here's my answer, and I think you're going to dig it!

Trust Thy SELF above all

For years, we are taught to trust in something or someone outside of ourselves, yet we often discover that even the most loving and well-meaning people or scenarios that make great sense on paper do not always result in our journey of choice. After a few iffy or painful experiences, it's no wonder that we sometimes find ourselves highly reluctant to delegate when we're overwhelmed, unwilling to take any kind of risks and hesitant to explore the unknown. When we live this kind of guarded life, however, we greatly limit our ability to experience joy and rarely Allow any kind of lasting success in any area of life.

Here's the GOOD news: When you discover that you absolutely CAN trust the guidance that comes from within—in the form of what feels right in your gut—you begin to experience a level of freedom that enhances your life and Allowing ability to the MAX! By taking the pressure off of others to perpetually "straighten up and fly right" in order for you to feel good, you experience the bonus of having more joy-filled relationships Allowing a much better journey for all involved!

Even though I am blessed to know many wonderful people who love me and want the best for me, I have learned that only I can ever truly know what is best for ME at any particular moment. Every time I go with what my gut tells me—even when it does not seem to make any logical sense to anyone else around me—I ALWAYS find myself in or on the way to Allowing what I truly want. It is only when I ignore or disregard my feelings in favor of some outside set of facts or opinions from others that I found myself in funkytown!

Any time I have caught myself being overly concerned about how I think others may perceive me or my actions, I take a cue from Dr. Seuss: "Those who mind don't matter and those who matter don't mind."

I have truly found that all of the relationships I value deeply in my life, including individuals and clients who have been a part of my business and career-related success have all been people who "...don't mind."

Remember, the journey IS the destination, so honoring your own inner guidance, putting your trust in YOU and what feels good and right to YOU is a sure way to enjoy the journey and invite some fabulous fellow travelers along for the ride!

Trust the Gift of the Present

When you are fully present, or even better, in a state of appreciation of your NOW, there is no greater sense of peace or security. As a bonus, the more aware you are of how you feel now, the more in-tune you become with your body (and gut), Allowing you to choose and act CONSCIOUSLY rather than unconsciously. You can feel when your energy increases at the thought of something versus when your body tenses up. You begin to get a great sense of whether the thought you are thinking is moving you toward or away from something you truly want. Taking it a step further, when you fully quiet your mind, you get the added bonus of getting to know, feel and experience who you really are and connect with your Source, taking yourself beyond trusting into BEING.

Boost your TF (Trust Factor) by revisiting the good stuff!

As mentioned in Chapter 2, The Power of PRESENCE, if you are going to do a little time-traveling, choose the times and experiences that reinforce your **TF** (**T**rust **F**actor). Put them in writing, especially the times when you really wanted something and had no clue how it would all go down— and then it DID! Here's an example:

At one point in my life after investing quite a few years in the sales industry, I knew in my gut it was time to move on to fully focus on my passion for music. Even though I did not have any real financial guarantees waiting for me (at the time I was averaging $50-$100 per show and working 2-3 weekends a month), something inside me felt like it was time to make that leap, so I put in my two-week's notice. Only a few weeks of after *quitting my sales job, I was offered a 5-6 night per week gig fronting a high-energy dance band, which easily covered my bottom line, and then some!*

Trust, Courage and Resolve

Once you get clear about what you TRULY, MADLY, DEEPLY want, put it in writing and stick to it! One of the ways we can fall short of getting what we truly want, delay our true heart's desires or go on a trip we were not necessarily meaning to take is to vacillate or compromise our dreams downward. Why, oh why, would we ever do a silly thing like that? Speaking from experience, it's easy to get caught up in what may appear to be the only options at the time and choose based on what is in front of us, rather than what we truly want. But when I look back on my life, EVERY time I have Allowed something utterly magnificent, it has always been a case of putting my foot down and deciding that I WANT WHAT I WANT AND THAT'S WHAT I WANT! PERIOD!

Do understand that I certainly believe that being flexible is a good thing for many occasions, particularly when it comes to the extraneous details and the *how* part of letting our goodies in, but when you absolutely KNOW what you want in your heart-of-hearts and it is clear to you beyond ANY doubt, STICK TO YOUR GUNS! What do resolve and courage have to do with trust? When you have clearly entered a destination into your GPS and know where you are going, you can KNOW that any guidance you receive IS going to lead you there! Here are some examples:

My husband, John, had been married twice and had an extended run of dating women who would soon get back together with their ex-boyfriends. After sorting through enough of this contrast, John decided once and for all that, "I want the fairy tale! I want happily-ever-after and I want a woman to love me as much as I love her. Unless I can have that, I'd rather just be alone." (Yes, a hetero male actually said this!)

It was a little over a year after he declared this that he and I started dating, married and have been living happily ever after!!! On my side, I also decided once and for all that I wanted my prince-charming-soul-mate-happily-ever-after or nothing else, so I dare say it worked to BOTH of our advantages!

Here's another more recent example:

Just before the end of 2010, I declared a very specific and clear intention that I would focus on doing the things I love and leave the deliberate marketing, sales and bookings to wonderful people who LOVE doing what they do, who know and believe in the value and vision of what I have to offer and who would enjoy sharing the wealth together. Knowing that the journey IS the destination, I only work with people and participate in experiences that I ENJOY.

Shortly after gaining this clarity, I was soon to be taking part in an event that I had been extremely excited about, which was actually part of the inspiration to declare this intention to begin with! About a week before the event, a few things popped up that would require me to act in a way that was completely opposite of my intentions, so rather than ignore my gut and go ahead, I decided to trust myself and stand my ground by gracefully opting out, even though the event was close at hand and there could potentially be some negative repercussions.

After acting on this decision, the most extraordinary things happened! The organizer and my fellow presenters totally honored and respected my decision, so my withdrawal was completely peaceful! The NEXT DAY I was offered a show that would be happening on the SAME DAY as the event I had opted out of, which then connected me to some of the finest musicians I have worked with to date, that then resulted in several MONTHS worth of repeat bookings and new business (which brought me FAR more revenue than I would have made at the one day event!). As a result of my new schedule and material, my voice and performance level also easily and naturally evolved to a whole new level of excellence! Needless to say, I had all the proof I needed to know that I had made the right decision!

By TRUSTING that I could have what I truly wanted and backing it up with the willingness to stand my ground, boy did life deliver!

What is it that you KNOW you truly want?

The Two-For-One Special: Trust you to be you and them to be them and everyone wins!

When it comes to interacting with other people, only one thing is certain: Everyone is doing what is best for them at that moment in time. Even the most giving and caring people on the planet who seem to do all they can to help and take care of everyone else are still doing whatever THEY feel is best at the time. Any time my husband and I have played the "I'll-do-what-I-think-he/she-wants" guessing-game and neither of us followed our own guidance, the results were NEVER pretty. It really was like the cliché of "the blind leading the blind!"

When you fully understand that everyone is doing what feels best to them in the moment and you stay in the habit of acting on what feels good and right for you, you end up enjoying your journey, sharing the ideal words and engaging in the best actions at the right time to be of the greatest benefit to anyone on the receiving end!

The Bottom Line on The Power of TRUST

When you embrace a life of TRUST:

> **T**ruth and freedom can be found.
> **R**eality breaks new ground.
> **U**nderstanding becomes profound.
> **S**ynchronicity and serendipity abound.
> **T**ime spent enjoying the journey is Allowed!

I TRUST you got the message?!

—

*"A little faith a little trust can carry me through anything,
so I let them come to me, all those infinite possibilities..."*

From "Infinite Possibilities"
© 2007-11 T.T.R.H.

The Power of TRUST: Allowing Power Tools

*Ready to rev-up your **TF** (Trust Factor)? Here are a few T-riffic tools:*

Remember, for best results, focus on the tools that feel best to you now
(= give you a lighter feeling or sense of relief).

TOOL#1
TRUST THE GIFT OF THE PRESENT

Now IS something you can count on!

———◆———

DO THIS:

When you want to get in touch with your inner guidance, create consciously and remember who you truly are

1.   Revisit any of the tools in Chapter 2, The Power of PRESENCE.

TOOL#2
REPLAY THE TRUST TAPES

*Boost you **TF** by revisting the good stuff*

———◆———

DO THIS:

When you need a reminder of just how fabulous you are and how well things go when you trust your inner guidance!

1. Choose times and experiences (even recalling events that may have happened that same day) that reinforce your TF and put them in writing.

On a daily basis, or as needed, note times when you had a hunch to do something (or not), followed your guidance, and it turned out beautifully!

On a daily basis, or as needed, revisit past experiences when you really wanted something and had no clue how it would all go down, but then it DID!

TOOL#3
DECIDE, THEN STAND YOUR GROUND

A little courage and resolve goes a long way!

DO THIS:

When you feel abundantly clear about something you truly want and really want to focus upon the having/living of it

1. Revisit TOOL#4: FOCUSED INTENTION in Chapter 7, The Power of OWNERSHIP.

Declare a clear intention that makes your heart sing!

2. Revisit TOOL#2: THE HEART OF THE MATTER in Chapter 6, The Power of AUTHENTICITY.

Get to the true heart of your desire and connect with the overall feeling-experience you are reaching for.

3. Expect and know that is it DONE and accept only what truly feels right-on to you!

Accept nothing less than what you truly want because you know you are a **CEO** and CAN have it!!

The Power of Words:
Trust Talk

A great way to cultivate The Power of TRUST?
TALK the (TRUST) TALK!

Instead of Worrisome Words	Use Trust Talk
I can't trust anyone to do things right. As usual, I just need to do it all myself.	I really like knowing that when I trust my gut, I find the right help at the right time to do the job well.
You really can't count on anyone. People are flaky!	I've noticed that when I'm feeling good about myself and am clear about what I want, great people show up.
I can't see how things could possibly be different.	I've seen so many examples of positive changes occur throughout my life that I know there are infinite possibilities for my dreams to come to me!
Trust no one and no one will let you down.	When I trust myself first and foremost, no one can ever let me down.

The Power of Music for TRUST

Download music for The Power of TRUST
by visiting this link: www.AllowingYourSuccess.com/SecretPages

- ☛ Then use the code AYS-tjitd
- ☛ Then choose ALLOWING Music
- ☛ Then The Power of TRUST
- ☛ Then click on the song title of your choosing and ENJOY!

*Thank you in advance for honoring and respecting the value of our work and using this code just for you and your household.

Additional Resources for
The Power of TRUST

Movies, Books & Beyond:

Star Trek (new version, film)

'Round Ireland with a Fridge (film)

August Rush (film)

Finding Nemo (film)

Indigo (film)

Mame (film-musical – my fave version stars Lucile Ball)

The Celestine Prophecy film and book series by James Redfield

SoundsTrue.com (multiple titles, authors and resources)

Shambhala.com (multiple titles, authors and resources)

HayHouse.com (multiple titles, authors and resources)

Transformation-Publishing.com (multiple titles, authors and resources)

Allowing Evidence Series:
http://AllowingYourSuccess.com/true_stories.php

To access our current list of ever-expanding resources visit:
http://AllowingYourSuccess.com/allowing_resources.php

<u>Your Journey So Far:</u>

FOCUS
on the PRESENCE
of the BEAUTY
of your true NATURE
with APPRECIATION
for your AUTHENTICITY
as you take OWNERSHIP of your joy
and live life in HARMONY
as a magnificent EXPRESSION
of good HUMOR
and TRUST.

12. The Power of ADVENTURE: Allowing Keys

LIFE is THE ultimate Allowing Adventure!

Life at a higher level

Congratulations for making it this far in your journey of Allowing Your Success!

When you start to truly taste what a life of Allowing is like, you begin to live at a higher level. You begin to believe that magic IS real and that life IS magnificent. You move through life as if everyone you meet and every experience you engage in was placed just for you. Every sense is heightened and every exchange and interaction become more and more meaningful and joyful. Life becomes more of the FUN ADVENTURE it was meant to be. Just as promised in the introduction of this book, once you set upon the path of Allowing success, a monochromatic lens and experience of life no longer satisfies. Living out loud in Technicolor® and feeling truly alive, however, certainly make the upgrade well worth the trip!

Adventure and the BPI

Few things have the power to bring us into an Allowing state of mind like fully aligning with the spirit of ADVENTURE! The thrill of seeing, doing or experiencing something fresh and new—particularly something we have deliberately chosen—is an ultra-fabulous way to get our Allowing juices flowing whether we are:

- exploring a new travel destination.
- taking a new route to work.
- moving into a new home.
- trying food or beverages we have never sampled before.
- creating a new website.
- changing our look.
- becoming parents for the first time.
- choosing to embark upon a new vocation.

Considering that the **BPI** (**B**ig **P**icture **I**ntention) is all about enjoying the journey while expanding your life and SELF into new places, it's no wonder that participating in adventure feels SO very good! I know, for example, when I have traveled to a place I have never been or hiked a new trail, all my senses become heightened and I am fully present and aware. My desire and ability to focus on beauty while appreciating where I am and what I am doing just come with the territory! So the fact that The Power of ADVENTURE can include ALL of our ALLOWING Power Tools:

- The Power of FOCUS
- The Power of PRESENCE
- The Power of BEAUTY
- The Power of NATURE
- The Power of APPRECIATION
- The Power of AUTHENTICITY
- The Power of OWNERSHIP
- The Power of HARMONY
- The Power of EXPRESSION
- The Power of HUMOR
- The Power of TRUST

...makes it one HECK of an A-List Allowing Power Tool!

Embracing Adventure means getting to enjoy the journey NOW

Here's another great reason to embrace and incorporate The Power of ADVENTURE into your Allowing repertoire: You get to ENJOY the journey NOW, rather than wait with bated breath for your stuff to make its way to you before you can be happy, or continue to stop and take score (which actually keeps a vibration of "It's not here, I don't have it." alive and well).

Participating in some kind of happy adventure today and NOW Allows you to ENJOY now, which IS what having our stuff/experiences is ALL about any way! During the time you are actively and fully engaged in enjoying your adventure, you are also too busy to be worrying about what hasn't happened yet...

...meaning you are no longer resisting the flow of life and are Allowing!

It's just like the example in Chapter 9, The Power of EXPRESSION: When you discover you have lost something and then search like mad to find it, you rarely do. In contrast, if you step away for a while to do something completely unrelated (which shifts your vibe and emotional state), then, low and behold, right in front of you is the item you were so desperately searching for. This can also be the case for your DREAMS, VISIONS and INTENTIONS my friends!

At the same time, when you get into a flow of enjoying your day to day life and discover/create happy adventures just for the FUN of it—without any ulterior motive—you begin to realize that you no longer need anything to live the **BPI** and BE Successful, and your great adventure of life becomes truly magical!

Bonuses, happy surprises & upgrades!

Like the word TRUST, ADVENTURE also comes with many meanings. When it comes to Allowing, the name of the game is to use The Power of ADVENTURE as a tool for letting good happen and ENJOYING the journey! Instead of the old-school fear-based Deliverance-esque paradigm of facing potential danger, forcing ourselves to do something that is utterly terrifying, or persevering for the sake of conquering (AKA **HHW**), truly engaging The Power of ADVENTURE for our purposes means having a clear intent for fun and joy while opening ourselves up to (and expecting!) bonuses, happy surprises and upgrades!

In case I haven't made this point abundantly clear, engaging in FUN and deliberate adventures based on enjoying the journey and discovering fabulous new things and experiences is one of the ULTIMATE ways to fulfill the **BPI!**

Embrace The Power of ADVENTURE on YOUR terms

Like success, everyone has her or his own idea of what ADVENTURE means to them. From simply choosing a new nail polish color or attending a different sporting event to traveling solo overseas or hiking across the country, there is a level of adventure that is suitable for everyone. Regardless of what others may deem a worthy adventure, all that matters in the grand scheme of Allowing Your Success is what gives YOU a sense of joy in exploring something new that appeals to YOU.

Always remember this is YOUR success, YOUR adventure, and YOUR path we're talking about, baby!

The Bottom Line on The Power of ADVENTURE

Every adventure first begins with a point of focus and a choice.

Welcome, my friends, to the destination, and the continuing journey. You have come full circle since The Power of FOCUS and have indeed come a long way, baby! If you have read this book in its entirety and begun to directly and personally experience what Allowing Your Success feels like, you have stepped into a brave new world, a whole new level of evolution and a whole new state of being—but it doesn't stop here!

The great news is that life is an ever-expanding adventure, which will continue to be filled with new dreams and desires being identified and born within you with ongoing opportunities for you to continue to Allow a brighter, more beautiful and amazing version of YOU and your life!

By choosing to engage in the ultimate adventure of Allowing Your Success, you create not only a richer, more magnificent journey for yourself, but also a brighter and more powerful beacon of light that truly CAN light the way for others. You also contribute to creating a world that your children and children's children will thank YOU for, for generations to come!

On behalf of every fellow traveler on this planet having the human adventure, I honor and appreciate you more than words can say.

Wishing you all the best—and Beyond!!

Onward and Upward!!!

Terez

"...Today I experience the greatest adventure of my life!
I move forward with confidence, following the stars in my sky,
for I know that where I go and where I am is always, always right..."

from "Being the Destination"
© 2004-12 T.T.R.H.

The Power of ADVENTURE:
Allowing Power Tools

Here are some amazing tools for engaging the Allowing-tabulous Power of ADVENTURE:

Remember, for best results, focus on the tools that feel best to you now
(= give you a lighter feeling or sense of relief).

TOOL#1
ADVENTURE IN YOUR BACK YARD

Even ordinary, day to day life can hold adventures, if you Allow them!

DO THIS:

When you want to get your Allowing wheels turning and experience the excitement of discovering something new!

1. Make a list of things you could do to add a sense of adventure to your day-to-day life.

2. Keep this list handy (via posting it on your fridge, keeping it on your phone/iPad or in your wallet) and choose at least one adventure weekly, daily or ANY time you'd like to add more FUN to your life!

Here are a few ideas to get you started:

Gastronomic Adventures: Spice up your life! The next time you go grocery shopping or cook, try a different combination of spices, or a beverage that you've never tried before.

Outdoor Adventures: Remember the Supertramp song, "Take the Long Way Home"?

On your way home from work/meeting/shopping/dropping off the kids, drive through that neat-looking neighborhood you've always wanted to check out, or opt for taking the more scenic road. Because it may be rush hour, why not even choose to park the car and stroll through one of those neighborhoods for a few minutes?

Indoor Adventures: Paint at least one wall in your home a color that you really love.

Adventures in Friendship: Join a class or interest-oriented Meetup group in your area www.Meetup.com

You can also join our local "Law of Attraction Music, Media and Events" group (free) and be a part of one of our fun Allowing-oriented events by visiting: http://www.meetup.com/lawofattraction-335/

Adventures in Love: Write love notes and leave them in places your sweetheart will find later like in pockets, in her/his vehicle, attached to her/his phone/computer, etc.

For a personal example of this tool in action visit:
www.AllowingYourSuccess.com/SecretPages

- ☞ Then use the code AYS-tjitd
- ☞ Then choose ALLOWING Power Tools
- ☞ Then The Power of ADVENTURE
- ☞ Then TOOL#1: ADVENTURE IN YOUR BACK YARD

TOOL#2
EMBRACE ADVENTURE ON A LARGER SCALE

"The mountains are calling and I must go."

~John Muir~

DO THIS:

When you want to get your Allowing wheels turning and experience the excitement of discovering something new!

1. Think BIG and make a list of the grander adventures you'd like to participate in that could rock your world in beautiful ways!

2. Live the adventure and enjoy the journey NOW!

Take that road trip. Book that vacation/retreat. Hike the Appalachian Trail. Take that class. Learn that language. Sail. Move to that other city, state or country. Start that business or that book or that piece or...

Choosing to give yourself the gift of a truly great adventure is an awesome way to directly fulfill the **BPI** and fully LIVE right NOW.

When we wait to live, we live to wait – so why not do it NOW?

If you love the idea of traveling to magical, beautiful destinations while focusing on Allowing success with fun, like-minded fellow travelers, join us for our next "Allowing Adventure!" retreat experience!

For details and info about the next adventure destination visit: www.AllowingAdventures.com

The Power of Words:
Adventurous Aphorisms

Prime your life for adventure by expanding your language to boldly go where you have never gone before!

Instead of Routine Rhetoric	Use Adventurous Aphorisms
I don't have time for adventure...	There are all kinds of opportunities for adventure, even in my day-to-day life.
Adventures are risky and dangerous.	Choosing an adventure that I want is what makes life worth living!
Sure I'd have adventures if I had tons of cash, was younger, was an athlete, blah, blah, blah...	Adventure can be had on any budget, on any day, at every age and at any time.
It's better to just stick with what I know and do what others before me have done for ages.	I love the idea of my life experience being something extraordinary, going beyond what's already been done and getting to the end of this life having truly enjoyed my journey. Now that's what I call leaving a legacy!

The Power of Music for ADVENTURE

Download music for The Power of ADVENTURE
by visiting this link: www.AllowingYourSuccess.com/SecretPages

- ☞ Then use the code AYS-tjitd
- ☞ Then choose ALLOWING Music
- ☞ Then The Power of ADVENTURE
- ☞ Then click on the song title of your choosing and ENJOY!

*Thank you in advance for honoring and respecting the value of our work and using this code just for you and your household.

Additional Resources for
The Power of ADVENTURE

Movies, Books & Beyond:

Star Trek (new version - film)

'Round Ireland with a Fridge (film)

August Rush (film)

Finding Nemo (film)

Opa! (film)

Coming to America (film)

Uncross the Stars (film)

Under the Tuscan Sun (film)

Whatever Lola Wants (film)

Mame (film-musical – my fave version with Lucile Ball)

Galaxy Quest (film)

Romancing the Stone (film)

Shall We Dance? (film)

The Sound of Music (film)

Splash (film)

Wall-E (film)

The Celestine Prophecy film and book series by James Redfield

SoundsTrue.com (multiple titles, authors and resources)

Additonal Resources for
The Power of ADVENTURE (continued)

Shambhala.com (multiple titles, authors and resources)

HayHouse.com (multiple titles, authors and resources)

Transformation-Publishing.com (multiple titles, authors and resources)

Any great adventure story that moves and inspires you!

SpiritualCinemaCircle.com

Chinanet.org (exchange student hosting program)

Geocaching.com

Couchsurfing.com
(meet people from all over the globe by "surfing" or hosting!)

Meetup.com

AllowingAdventures.com

To access our current list of ever-expanding resources visit:
http://AllowingYourSuccess.com/allowing_resources.php

<u>Your Journey!</u>

FOCUS
on the PRESENCE
of the BEAUTY
of your true NATURE
with APPRECIATION
for your AUTHENTICITY
as you take OWNERSHIP of your joy
and live life in HARMONY
as a magnificent EXPRESSION
of good HUMOR -
and TRUST
in the ADVENTURE that is Life!

V.
Allowing Resources:

Movies, Books & BEYOND!

Glossary of Terms

About the Author

1. Movies, Books & BEYOND!: Additional Resources for ALLOWING Your Success!

The following is a list of all additional resources mentioned throughout the book, sorted by chapter/topic.

To access our current list of ever-expanding resources visit:
http://allowingyoursuccess.com/allowing_resources.php

SECTION III. ALLOWING FOUNDATION

Chapter 1 – The Law of Attraction:

What The Bleep Do We Know?
The science behind thought (quantum physics)
presented in a fun format
www.WhatTheBleep.com

The Secret
Created by Rhonda Byrne and featuring many of today's
Law of Attraction specialists
www.TheSecret.tv

The Secret Behind the Secret
DVD Featuring Abraham-Hicks
(the original inspiration behind the Secret –
only watch with an open mind)
www.Abraham-Hicks.com

You Can Heal Your Life
film featuring the work of Louise Hay
www.YouCanHealYourLifeMovie.com

The Law of Attraction audio series by Abraham-Hicks
www.Abraham-Hicks.com

Ask and it is Given book/audio by Abraham-Hicks
www.Abraham-Hicks.com

The Power of Intention book/audio by Dr. Wayne Dyer
www.DrWayneDyer.com

The Secret book/audio by Rhonda Byrne
www.TheSecret.tv

Notes From The Universe and *Infinite Possibilities*
books by Mike Dooley
www.Tut.com

As a Man Thinketh by James Allen

Think and Grow Rich by Napoleon Hill

The Science of Getting Rich by Wallace Wattles

Illusions by Richard Bach

SoundsTrue.com (multiple titles, authors and resources)

HayHouse.com (multiple titles, authors and resources)

Transformation-Publishing.com (multiple titles, authors and resources)

Chapter 2 – The Power of Words:

All books by Dr. Masaru Emoto

You Can Heal Your Life and many others by Louise Hay

The Four Agreements, Don Miguel Ruiz

Chapter 3 – The Power of Music:

A study of Designer Music:
http://www.heartmath.org/research/research-papers/effect-music-mood.html

SECTION IV. ALLOWING KEYS &
ALLOWING POWER TOOLS: POSITIVI-TS™

Chapter 1 – The Power of FOCUS:

All *Star Wars* films

Jillian's Vantage (short film)

That's Magic (short film)

August Rush (film)

Make Believe (film-a great comparison of Old School/New School)

Emmanuel's Gift* (film-documentary)

All and any books, audio books or DVDs by Abraham-Hicks

The Best Year of Your Life – Debbie Ford

The Power of Intention – Dr. Wayne Dyer

The Seven Spiritual Laws of Success – Deepak Chopra

Living Juicy – Sark

SoundsTrue.com (multiple titles, authors and resources)

Shambhala.com (multiple titles, authors and resources)

HayHouse.com (multiple titles, authors and resources)

Transformation-Publishing.com (multiple titles, authors and resources)

**Contains some not-so-pretty footage in places but this true story of
a living human being is an astounding testimony of The Power of FOCUS.*

Chapter 2 – The Power of PRESENCE:

Peaceful Warrior, based on the novel by Dan Millman (film)

Forrest Gump (film)

Getting Into The Vortex, Book and Meditation CD by Abraham-Hicks

The Power of Now and *A New Earth* by Eckhart Tolle

ZEN 24/7, by Phillip Toshio Sudo

Way of the Peaceful Warrior, by Dan Millman

8 Minute Meditation, by Victor Davich

Big Mind – Big Heart, by Dennis Genpo Merzel

Accelerated Meditation DVD—Part of the World Wealth 2008 series, available through jamesray.com (phenomenal and transformational)

The Sedona Method – Sedona.com

SoundsTrue.com (multiple titles, authors and resources)

Shambhala.com (multiple titles, authors and resources)

HayHouse.com (multiple titles, authors and resources)

Transformation-Publishing.com (multiple titles, authors and resources)

Observe nature, your pet, or young children.
They are all great "Zen Masters!"

Chapter 3 – The Power of BEAUTY:

Maryanne Goes to The Market (short film)

Avatar (film with stunning visual effects!)

Chocolat (film featuring beauty through chocolate!)

A Not So Still Life (film-documentary about
the amazing journey of artist Ginny Ruffner)

· *Opa!* (film with beautiful footage of Greece)

Any book, film or music that highlights beauty in ANY form

SoundsTrue.com (multiple titles, authors and resources)

Shambhala.com (multiple titles, authors and resources)

HayHouse.com (multiple titles, authors and resources)

Transformation-Publishing.com (multiple titles, authors and resources)

PeterLik.com (astoundingly beautiful photography)

Andre Desjardins
("visual emotion-ism," the Da Vinci or Michelangelo of our time—wow!)

SigridTidmore.com (images to awaken the mind)

Roy Vance: yessy.com/roysart
(beautiful modern art paired with positive intentions)

Afsaneh's Art: ChangeThrivers.com
(hand painted, hand-picked, one-of-a-kind snail shells)

Chapter 4 – The Power of NATURE:

The Emerald Forest (film)

Avatar (film)

Brother Bear (film)

Animal Speak by Ted Andrews

Power Animals by Steven D. Farmer

SoundsTrue.com (multiple titles, authors and resources)

Shambhala.com (multiple titles, authors and resources)

HayHouse.com (multiple titles, authors and resources)

Transformation-Publishing.com (multiple titles, authors and resources)

Get OUT and watch the best show on earth:
Go for a hike, paddle, stroll or climb in a beautiful natural place
near you!

Visit county, state and national parks

Chapter 5 – The Power of APPRECIATION:

Charlie and The Chocolate Factory (film)

Delivering Milo (film)

Beauty and the Beast (film)

The Man Who Never Cried (short film)

That's Magic (short film)

Gratitude (short film)

SoundsTrue.com (multiple titles, authors and resources)

Shambhala.com (multiple titles, authors and resources)

HayHouse.com (multiple titles, authors and resources)

Transformation-Publishing.com (multiple titles, authors and resources)

Share Appreciation! Visit www.SendOutCards.com
A great online greeting card company that I like to use that makes
sharing appreciation convenient, easy and fun

Watch a baby or young child smile, laugh and fully engage
with some fascinating toy, object or food item! Talk about appreciation!

Chapter 6 – The Power of AUTHENTICITY:

Under the Tuscan Sun (film)

Cool Runnings (film)

Chocolate (film)

Swing (film)

Taos (film)

Living Luminaries (film)

Opa! (film)

5 Wishes (short film)

August Rush (film)

The Shift: Ambition to Meaning (film)

The Celestine Prophecy (film)

5 Wishes by Gay Hendricks

Jonathan Livingston Seagull by Richard Bach

The Passion Test by Janet Bray Attwood and Chris Attwood

Dandelion by Sheelagh Mawe

SoundsTrue.com (multiple titles, authors and resources)

Shambhala.com (multiple titles, authors and resources)

HayHouse.com (multiple titles, authors and resources)

Transformation-Publishing.com (multiple titles, authors and resources)

Your gut and inner guidance—THE best Authenticity gauge, EVER!

Chapter 7 – The Power of OWNERSHIP:

August Rush (film)

Cool Runnings (film)

Field of Dreams (film)

The Perfect Game (film)

Kung Fu Panda (film)

The Matrix (film)

The Wizard of Oz (film-musical)

Any book, DVD or audio book by Abraham-Hicks

The Life-Visioning Process (audio) by Michael Bernard Beckwith

Illusions by Richard Bach

The Circle by Laura Day

The Best Year of Your Life by Debbie Ford

Living Juicy by Sark

SoundsTrue.com (multiple titles, authors and resources)

Shambhala.com (multiple titles, authors and resources)

HayHouse.com (multiple titles, authors and resources)

Transformation-Publishing.com (multiple titles, authors and resources)
MastermindU.com - a great site for Mastermind resources

AllowingAdventures.com – Allowing, Mastermind and travel!

Chapter 8 – The Power of HARMONY:

Broken Hill (film)

August Rush (film)

My Big Fat Greek Wedding (film)

Sabah (film)

Secrets of Six-Figure Women by Barbara Stanny

True Balance by Sonia Choquette

SoundsTrue.com (multiple titles, authors and resources)

Shambhala.com (multiple titles, authors and resources)

HayHouse.com (multiple titles, authors and resources)

Transformation-Publishing.com (multiple titles, authors and resources)

Virtually any song or piece of music by Enya

Rockapella, a killer a capella vocal group!

Any music that makes your heart soar!

Chapter 9 – The Power of EXPRESSION:

All movies and books mentioned in this book plus:

Conversations with God (film) - EI and ER

The Moses Code (film-documentary) – EI

One (film-documentary) – EI

Black Whole (film-documentary, fascinating and inspiring!) – EI

Listen to Your Heart (film) – EI and ER

The Artist's Way by Julia Cameron – EI and ER

Conversations with God series of books
by Neale Donald Walsch – EI

Chicken Soup for the Soul series
by Jack Canfield and Mark Victor Hansen – EI and ER

All books, audio programs or DVDs by Abraham-Hicks - EI

All books by Og Mandino – EI and ER

All books by John Harricharan – EI and ER

All books by Deepak Chopra – EI (some ER)

All books by Wayne Dyer – EI (some ER)

SoundsTrue.com (multiple titles, authors and resources) – EI and ER

Shambhala.com (multiple titles, authors and resources) – EI and ER

HayHouse.com (multiple titles, authors and resources) – EI and ER

Transformation-Publishing.com
(multiple titles, authors and resources) – EI and ER

Mike Dooley's "Notes From The Universe"
www.tut.com/resources/notes/
(inspiring daily e-mails) – EI

DailyWord.com (daily inspiration from Unity) – EI

VenusJones.com (stirring spoken word artist and poet) – EI and ER

MoxyWomen.com
(site dedicated to empowering and inspiring women) – EI and ER

The Out Your ego! Series – divination cards, book, board game
www.StaciB.com – EI and ER

SpiritualCinemaCircle.com
(monthly film club that brings inspirational films with
heart and soul to your door!) – EI and ER

AllowingYourSuccess.com
(words, music, adventures and beyond dedicated to Allowing) – EI

Music – for all reasons and seasons! EI and ER

Chapter 10 – The Power of HUMOR:

Shrek (film, entire film series)

The Producers (film)

Cheaper by the Dozen (films)

The American Pie Series (film)

The Birdcage (film)

The Hangover (film)

Bill & Ted's Excellent Adventure (film)

Trading Places (film)

Cool Runnings (film)

The Wedding Singer (film)

Wayne's World (film)

The *Austin Powers* series of films

Van Wilder (film)

Abbot & Costello series of films

SoundsTrue.com (multiple titles, authors and resources)

Shambhala.com (multiple titles, authors and resources)

HayHouse.com (multiple titles, authors and resources)

Transformation-Publishing.com (multiple titles, authors and resources)

Seriously... I'm Kidding audio book by Ellen DeGeneres

Jeff Dunham - comedian

The Blue Collar Comedy Tour

Louis Black - comedian

Gabrielle Inglesias - comedian

Bill Cosby - comedian

Robin Williams - comedian

Weird-Al – song parodies
(my personal favorite parodies are "Amish Paradise,"
"All About the Pentium," "White and Nerdy")

Whose Line is it Anyway? TV show hosted by Drew Carey— hilarious!!

Comedy Central

BBC Comedy

Chapter 11 – The Power of TRUST:

Star Trek (new version, film)

'Round Ireland with a Fridge (film)

August Rush (film)

Finding Nemo (film)

Indigo (film)

Mame (film-musical – my fave version stars Lucile Ball)

The Celestine Prophecy film and book series by James Redfield

SoundsTrue.com (multiple titles, authors and resources)

Shambhala.com (multiple titles, authors and resources)

HayHouse.com (multiple titles, authors and resources)

Transformation-Publishing.com (multiple titles, authors and resources)

Allowing Evidence Series:
http://AllowingYourSuccess.com/true_stories.php

Chapter 12 – The Power of ADVENTURE:

Star Trek (new version - film)

'Round Ireland with a Fridge (film)

August Rush (film)

Finding Nemo (film)

Opa! (film)

Coming to America (film)

Uncross the Stars (film)

Under the Tuscan Sun (film)

Whatever Lola Wants (film)

Mame (film-musical – my fave version with Lucile Ball)
Galaxy Quest (film)

Romancing the Stone (film)

Shall We Dance? (film)

The Sound of Music (film)

Splash (film)

Wall-E (film)

The Celestine Prophecy film and book series by James Redfield

SoundsTrue.com (multiple titles, authors and resources)

Shambhala.com (multiple titles, authors and resources)

HayHouse.com (multiple titles, authors and resources)

Transformation-Publishing.com (multiple titles, authors and resources)

Any great adventure story that moves and inspires you!

SpiritualCinemaCircle.com

Chinanet.org (exchange student hosting program)

Geocaching.com

Couchsurfing.com
(meet people from all over the globe by "surfing" or hosting!)

Meetup.com

AllowingAdventures.com

2. Glossary of Terms

A

AKA: Also Known As.

Alignment: being at one, in harmony or in sync with something or a state of being.

Allowing: letting good happen, receiving.

Allowing Adventures!: Terez's retreat and travel series - www.AllowingAdventures.com

Allowing-tabulous: Allowing + fantastic + fabulous.

All-Things-Fabulous: anything synonymous with the good stuff for you.

Angry Chef: the opposite of the Happy Chef—an example of resistance.

B

Bling: shiny objects, toys, or any fabulous things that represent wealth and prosperity.

Bob: an example of an awesome appreciator.

BPI: Big Picture Intention: "I am LOVING ME and having a GREAT TIME while BECOMING MORE!"

C

CEO: Creator, Experiencer, Opener.

Creator: an aspect of being a CEO and what every living human being is—the creator of her/his life experience.

D

Destination: the journey in and of itself, sometimes disguised as our desired result, intention, bling, etc.

E

EI: Express to Increase.

ER: Express to Release.

Evolution Revolution: leading edge change and expansion.

Experiencer: An aspect of being a CEO and what every living human being is; the one who experiences whatever s/he has been creating.

F

Fabulousness: awesomeness, greatness.

Focused Intention: a clear and specific intention/goal.

Funky: good, when referring to music with a great groove.

Funky: icky when referring to unpleasant things.

Funkytown: An undesirable destination, not be be confused with the super-cool song, "Funkytown" by Lipps Inc.

G

Groovy-er: groovy, as in way cool, man, but even cooler!

H

Happy Chef: example of the fabulousness of doing what you love.

I

Intention: desire, vision, dream, target, focal point.

J

Journey: our true destination, what we are doing and experiencing right now or on the way to harmonizing/aligning with an intention.

L

LOA : The Law of Attraction (discussed in detail in Section III, Chapter 1)

<lol!>: e-mail or texting term meaning "laugh out loud"

M

Mastermind Groups: a group of like-minded people who come together with the intention of inspiring each other and expanding thought, ideas, opportunities or intentions to a bigger, more powerful place (term originally referenced by Napoleon Hill in the book *Think and Grow Rich*).

N

Not-so-much: not so good, so-so, or even funky.

O

Opener: An aspect of being a CEO and what every living human being is; the one who opens the door/Allows (or not) her/his intentions and true self.

P

Par-tay: a super, hip cool way of saying "party!"

POP: Power of Presence.

POP Factor: Something that connects you to the present moment.

Positivi-Ts: Terez's Allowing Power Tools, also the title of her blog on www.AllowingYourSuccess.com.

Props: proper recognition.

Q

Quantum Physics: also called Quantum Theory or Quantum mechanics, the study of the behavior of matter and energy at the molecular, atomic, nuclear, and even smaller microscopic levels. Quantum Physics studies are highlighted in the book and movie *What The Bleep Do We Know?* and *Black Whole*.

R

RDA: Recommended Daily Allowance.

REP: Repeating Emotional Pattern.

The River: A state of being where you immerse yourself fully and completely in whatever emotions you are feeling without judgment or limitation in order to express and release negative emotions.

Resistance: The opposite of Allowing, blocking or slowing down the process of Allowing.

S
Small Slices: mini-intentions, our intention for each action/experience we participate in. Abraham-Hicks calls this "segment intending" or "pre-paving."

Source: a general term used to represent Divine intelligence, an expanded experience of self or underlying universal connection.

Specialists: people you love and trust who can hold the "high ground" for you during ER sessions.

Success: enjoying the journey!

T
TF: Trust Factor.

U
über-tool: Super powerful tool!

Un-Bob: a copious complainer.

V
Vibe: short for vibration, AKA dominant emotional/mental state.

W
Whole Pie: Your personal big picture of your expanded version of all major aspects of your life, self and experiences including physical body/overall well-being, home, where and how you live, career/what you spend your time doing, stuff/experiences/adventures, and relationships.

Z
Zensational: Zen + sensational = being in a sensational state of presence.

3. About the Author

From the time she was a child, Thérèse "Terez" Tami Romano Hartmann was passionate about finding ways to help people to remember how powerful they truly are.

Even prior to the recent Law of Attraction movement, Terez spent the majority of her life consciously working with the Law of Attraction and Allowing, and owes her many years of ever-increasing professional success, her constant flow of creativity, her vibrant health, her many extraordinary adventures, her amazing relationships with positive-minded, cream-of-the-crop human beings and what she feels to be her greatest Allowing achievement, her extraordinary soul-mate marriage, to truly practicing what she teaches in her writings, presentations and music.

As a dynamic keynote speaker, singer-songwriter, recording and performing artist, entrepreneur, and visionary, her diverse range of material and abilities have allowed her to enjoy working in a wide variety of environments and with clients, venues and events ranging from Super Bowl XXXV – Coca-Cola, Xerox corporation, Walt Disney World and numerous national conventions, conferences and special events. She has received numerous awards and honors including a 2007 Tampa Bay Business Woman of the Year nomination, an FNI "Dream Achiever" award and a "Moxy Woman" award, granted by the International Association of Moxy Women (a designation shared with many living luminaries).

In addition to sharing her unique brand of "WORDS, MUSIC, ADVENTURES & BEYOND!" with individuals and organizations world-wide, Terez is a proud step-mom of three beautiful, independent spirits: Carey, Jackie and Sean. She has been a resident of Southern California, New York City and currently resides in Safety Harbor, Florida with her real-life-prince-charming husband, John and their two fabulous feline children Music and Magic.

For more about Terez, visit:
http://AllowingYourSuccess.com/about_terez.php

A personal message from Terez— the adventure continues...

Allowing the writing of this book has truly been one of the greatest successes of my life to date and, just as I emphasize throughout the book, I truly, fully and utterly enjoyed 100% of the journey! The information flowed seamlessly as if my completed book were already in existence, much like this great quote from Michelangelo: "I saw the angel in the marble and carved until I set him free..." and has only led and inspired me to the continuing adventures of discovering an entire series of books, workshops, retreats, music, blogs, an interview series and BEYOND!

If you would like to share in the ongoing adventure of Allowing Your Success! with me, visit the following links:

For all-things-Allowing including "WORDS, MUSIC, ADVENTURES and BEYOND for LETTING Good Happen and ENJOYING the Journey!", visit: www.AllowingYourSuccess.com

For info and updates about upcoming retreats and adventures focused on Allowing, visit:
www.AllowingAdventures.com

For an overview of my live presentations and services, visit:
www.TerezHartmann.LinkToExpert.com

My Facebook page:
www.facebook.com/TerezHartmann

My Meetup group:
www.meetup.com/lawofattraction-335/

To receive my monthly inspirational e-mail with Allowing insights, live appearance dates and BEYOND! e-mail this address with the subject "subscribe":
Info@AllowingYourSuccess.com

To listen to inspiring stories from real people who have Allowed success in many areas of life, visit:
http://www.allowingyoursuccess.com/true_stories.php

254

If YOU have a story of Allowing success or any other appreciation you'd like to share, e-mail: Story@AllowingYourSuccess.com

If you would like to bring one of my Keynotes or Workshops to your cutting-edge company or organization, e-mail:
Mgmt@AllowingYourSuccess.com

Wishing you all the Best – and BEYOND!!!

The Allowing Adventure Continues!

Join Terez, fellow Divine Deliberate Creators and Awesome Allowers for one (or all!) of our many **Allowing Adventures!** retreats as we LET Good Happen and ENJOY the Journey in some of the most beautiful, magical and spectacular places on earth! Because each destination is unique and we like to include up-to-the-minute Allowing stories, tools and music (in addition to Terez's quintessential Allowing Keys & Power Tools), all adventures are also unique and specifically designed to highlight and harmonize with the best of each location.

For details and info about upcoming Allowing Adventures! retreats, visit: www.AllowingAdventures.com

Photo by Lori Ballard

Special thanks to our 11-11-11 " Magic in the Red Rocks" Sedona, AZ Allowing Adventures! retreat participants and team (pictured left to right): Lori Ballard, Debby Kohler, Janie Boisclair, Tony "Saint Tone" Lavorgna, Sharon "Sharito" Steubi (and Damien), John Hartmann, Kate Mac Donald, Carol Mangan, Joanne Weiland, Christine Shea and Ficklin "Fick" Bryant.

256

Share YOUR "Allowing Evidence" and inspire others to Allow THEIR Success!

If YOU have an inspiring story about LETTING Good Happen while ENJOYING the Journey, Terez would love to hear from you!

For details and info about how YOU could be considered for an upcoming Allowing Evidence: Groovin' On LIFE! interview, visit

www.AllowingYourSuccess.com/true_stories.php
or send an e-mail to:
Story@AllowingYourSuccess.com

For all-things-Allowing including "WORDS, MUSIC, ADVENTURES and BEYOND!", visit www.AllowingYourSuccess.com

or scan the code below:

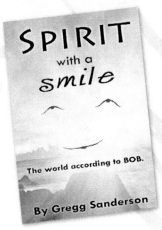

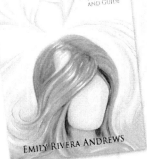